MznLnx

Missing Links Exam Preps

Exam Prep for

Calculus and Its Applications

Bittinger, 8th Edition

The MznLnx Exam Prep is your link from the texbook and lecture to your exams.
The MznLnx Exam Preps are unauthorized and comprehensive reviews of your textbooks.

All material provided by MznLnx and Rico Publications (c) 2010
Textbook publishers and textbook authors do not particpate in or contribute to these reviews.

MznLnx

Rico
Publications

Exam Prep for Calculus and Its Applications
8th Edition
Bittinger

Publisher: Raymond Houge
Assistant Editor: Michael Rouger
Text and Cover Designer: Lisa Buckner
Marketing Manager: Sara Swagger
Project Manager, Editorial Production: Jerry Emerson
Art Director: Vernon Lowerui

Product Manager: Dave Mason
Editorial Assitant: Rachel Guzmanji
Pedagogy: Debra Long
Cover Image: Jim Reed/Getty Images
Text and Cover Printer: City Printing, Inc.
Compositor: Media Mix, Inc.

(c) 2010 Rico Publications

ALL RIGHTS RESERVED. No part of this work covered by the copyright may be reproduced or used in any form or by an means--graphic, electronic, or mechanical, including photocopying, recording, taping, Web distribution, information storage, and retrieval systems, or in any other manner--without the written permission of the publisher.

Printed in the United States
ISBN:

For more information about our products, contact us at:
Dave.Mason@RicoPublications.com

For permission to use material from this text or product, submit a request online to:
Dave.Mason@RicoPublications.com

Contents

CHAPTER 1
Functions, Graphs, and Models   1

CHAPTER 2
Differentiation   32

CHAPTER 3
Applications of Differentiation   58

CHAPTER 4
Exponential and Logarithmic Functions   87

CHAPTER 5
Integration   114

CHAPTER 6
Applications of Integration   134

CHAPTER 7
Functions of Several Variables   157

ANSWER KEY   180

TO THE STUDENT

COMPREHENSIVE

The *MznLnx* Exam Prep series is designed to help you pass your exams. Editors at MznLnx review your textbooks and then prepare these practice exams to help you master the textbook material. Unlike study guides, workbooks, and practice tests provided by the texbook publisher and textbook authors, *MznLnx* gives you **all** of the material in each chapter in exam form, not just samples, so you can be sure to nail your exam.

MECHANICAL

The MznLnx Exam Prep series creates exams that will help you learn the subject matter as well as test you on your understanding. Each question is designed to help you master the concept. Just working through the exams, you gain an understanding of the subject--its a simple mechanical process that produces success.

INTEGRATED STUDY GUIDE AND REVIEW

MznLnx is not just a set of exams designed to test you, its also a comprehensive review of the subject content. Each exam question is also a review of the concept, making sure that you will get the answer correct without having to go to other sources of material. You learn as you go! Its the easiest way to pass an exam.

HUMOR

Studying can be tedious and dry. MznLnx's instructional design includes moderate humor within the exam questions on occassion, to break the tedium and revitalize the brain

Chapter 1. Functions, Graphs, and Models

1. In mathematics, a _____ is an expression that is constructed from one or more variables and constants, using only the operations of addition, subtraction, multiplication, and constant positive whole number exponents. is a _____. Note in particular that division by an expression containing a variable is not in general allowed in polynomials. [1]
    a. Thing
    b. Polynomial0
    c. Undefined
    d. Undefined

2. The mathematical concept of a _____ expresses the intuitive idea of deterministic dependence between two quantities, one of which is viewed as primary and the other as secondary. A _____ then is a way to associate a unique output for each input of a specified type, for example, a real number or an element of a given set.
    a. Thing
    b. Function0
    c. Undefined
    d. Undefined

3. In mathematics, a _____ of a k-place relation $L \subseteq X_1 \times ... \times X_k$ is one of the sets X_j, $1 \leq j \leq k$. In the special case where k = 2 and $L \subseteq X_1 \times X_2$ is a function $L : X_1 \to X_2$, it is conventional to refer to X_1 as the _____ of the function and to refer to X_2 as the codomain of the function.
    a. Thing
    b. Domain0
    c. Undefined
    d. Undefined

4. _____ are the basic objects of study in graph theory. Informally speaking, a graph is a set of objects called points, nodes, or vertices connected by links called lines or edges.
    a. Thing
    b. Graphs0
    c. Undefined
    d. Undefined

5. A _____ is an abstract model that uses mathematical language to describe the behavior of a system. Eykhoff defined a _____ as 'a representation of the essential aspects of an existing system which presents knowledge of that system in usable form'.

a. Mathematical model0
b. Thing
c. Undefined
d. Undefined

6. A _____ is a statement or claimt that a particular event will occur in the future in more certain terms than a forecast.
a. Thing
b. Prediction0
c. Undefined
d. Undefined

7. _____ is the fee paid on borrowed money.
a. Interest0
b. Thing
c. Undefined
d. Undefined

8. A _____ is a deliberate process for transforming one or more inputs into one or more results.
a. Calculation0
b. Thing
c. Undefined
d. Undefined

9. _____ interest refers to the fact that whenever interest is calculated, it is based not only on the original principal, but also on any unpaid interest that has been added to the principal.
a. Compound0
b. Thing
c. Undefined
d. Undefined

10. _____ refers to the fact that whenever interest is calculated, it is based not only on the original principal, but also on any unpaid interest that has been added to the principal. The more frequently interest is compounded, the faster the balance grows.

Chapter 1. Functions, Graphs, and Models

   a. Compound interest0
   b. Concept
   c. Undefined
   d. Undefined

11. _____ is the distance around a given two-dimensional object. As a general rule, the _____ of a polygon can always be calculated by adding all the length of the sides together. So, the formula for triangles is P = a + b + c, where a, b and c stand for each side of it. For quadrilaterals the equation is P = a + b + c + d. For equilateral polygons, P = na, where n is the number of sides and a is the side length.
   a. Thing
   b. Perimeter0
   c. Undefined
   d. Undefined

12. _____ is a branch of mathematics concerning the study of structure, relation and quantity.
   a. Algebra0
   b. Concept
   c. Undefined
   d. Undefined

13. _____ is a mathematical subject that includes the study of limits, derivatives, integrals, and power series and constitutes a major part of modern university curriculum.
   a. Calculus0
   b. Thing
   c. Undefined
   d. Undefined

14. A _____ is a set of numbers that designate location in a given reference system, such as x,y in a planar _____ system or an x,y,z in a three-dimensional _____ system.
   a. Coordinate0
   b. Thing
   c. Undefined
   d. Undefined

15. In astronomy, geography, geometry and related sciences and contexts, a plane is said to be _____ at a given point if it is locally perpendicular to the gradient of the gravity field, i.e., with the direction of the gravitational force at that point.

Chapter 1. Functions, Graphs, and Models

   a. Horizontal0
   b. Thing
   c. Undefined
   d. Undefined

16. A _____ is a symbolic representation denoting a quantity or expression. It often represents an "unknown" quantity that has the potential to change.
   a. Variable0
   b. Thing
   c. Undefined
   d. Undefined

17. An _____ is a collection of two not necessarily distinct objects, one of which is distinguished as the first coordinate and the other as the second coordinate.
   a. Ordered pair0
   b. Thing
   c. Undefined
   d. Undefined

18. In mathematics, the conjugate _____ or adjoint matrix of an m-by-n matrix A with complex entries is the n-by-m matrix A* obtained from A by taking the transpose and then taking the complex conjugate of each entry.
   a. Thing
   b. Pairs0
   c. Undefined
   d. Undefined

19. In mathematics, the concept of a _____ tries to capture the intuitive idea of a geometrical one-dimensional and continuous object. A simple example is the circle.
   a. Thing
   b. Curve0
   c. Undefined
   d. Undefined

20. In mathematics, _____ are the intuitive idea of a geometrical one-dimensional and continuous object.

a. Thing
b. Curves0
c. Undefined
d. Undefined

21. In mathematics, _____ geometry was the traditional name for the geometry of three-dimensional Euclidean space — for practical purposes the kind of space we live in.
a. Solid0
b. Thing
c. Undefined
d. Undefined

22. The _____ relates to the binary operation of multiplication and addition.
a. Thing
b. Distributive law0
c. Undefined
d. Undefined

23. In mathematics, the _____ is a conic section generated by the intersection of a right circular conical surface and a plane parallel to a generating straight line of that surface. It can also be defined as locus of points in a plane which are equidistant from a given point.
a. Parabola0
b. Thing
c. Undefined
d. Undefined

24. The word _____ comes from the Latin word linearis, which means created by lines.
a. Thing
b. Linear0
c. Undefined
d. Undefined

25. A _____ is an equation in which each term is either a constant or the product of a constant times the first power of a variable.

Chapter 1. Functions, Graphs, and Models

a. Linear equation0
b. Thing
c. Undefined
d. Undefined

26. In geographic information systems, a _____ comprises an entity with a geographic location, typically determined by points, arcs, or polygons. Carriageways and cadastres exemplify _____ data.
   a. Thing
   b. Feature0
   c. Undefined
   d. Undefined

27. In geometry, an _____ is a point at which a line segment or ray terminates.
   a. Endpoint0
   b. Thing
   c. Undefined
   d. Undefined

28. The _____ of measurement are a globally standardized and modernized form of the metric system.
   a. Units0
   b. Thing
   c. Undefined
   d. Undefined

29. An _____ is a straight line around which a geometric figure can be rotated.
   a. Thing
   b. Axis0
   c. Undefined
   d. Undefined

30. The _____, the average in everyday English, which is also called the arithmetic _____ (and is distinguished from the geometric _____ or harmonic _____). The average is also called the sample _____. The expected value of a random variable, which is also called the population _____.

a. Thing
b. Mean0
c. Undefined
d. Undefined

31. Mathematical _____ is used to represent ideas.
a. Notation0
b. Thing
c. Undefined
d. Undefined

32. In mathematics, _____ refers to a number of loosely related concepts in different areas of geometry. Intuitively, _____ is the amount by which a geometric object deviates from being flat, but this is defined in different ways depending on the context
a. Thing
b. Curvature0
c. Undefined
d. Undefined

33. In the scientific method, an _____ (Latin: ex-+-periri, "of (or from) trying"), is a set of actions and observations, performed in the context of solving a particular problem or question, in order to support or falsify a hypothesis or research concerning phenomena.
a. Experiment0
b. Thing
c. Undefined
d. Undefined

34. In sociology and biology a _____ is the collection of people or organisms of a particular species living in a given geographic area or space, usually measured by a census.
a. Population0
b. Thing
c. Undefined
d. Undefined

35. A _____ is a first degree polynomial mathematical function of the form: $f(x) = mx + b$ where m and b are real constants and x is a real variable.

a. Linear function0
b. Thing
c. Undefined
d. Undefined

36. A _____ is a unit of length, usually used to measure distance, in a number of different systems, including Imperial units, United States customary units and Norwegian/Swedish mil. Its size can vary from system to system, but in each is between 1 and 10 kilometers. In contemporary English contexts _____ refers to either:
    a. Mile0
    b. Thing
    c. Undefined
    d. Undefined

37. _____ is a kind of property which exists as magnitude or multitude. It is among the basic classes of things along with quality, substance, change, and relation.
    a. Amount0
    b. Thing
    c. Undefined
    d. Undefined

38. A _____ is a special kind of ratio, indicating a relationship between two measurements with different units, such as miles to gallons or cents to pounds.
    a. Thing
    b. Rate0
    c. Undefined
    d. Undefined

39. An _____ is the fee paid on borrow money.
    a. Concept
    b. Interest rate0
    c. Undefined
    d. Undefined

40. In mathematics, a _____ is a statement that can be proved on the basis of explicitly stated or previously agreed assumptions.

a. Theorem0
b. Thing
c. Undefined
d. Undefined

41. In geometry, the relations of _____ are those such as 'lies on' between points and lines (as in 'point P lies on line L'), and 'intersects' (as in 'line L_1 intersects line L_2', in three-dimensional space). That is, they are the binary relations describing how subsets meet.
  a. Incidence0
  b. Thing
  c. Undefined
  d. Undefined

42. A _____ is a type of debt. All material things can be lent but this article focuses exclusively on monetary loans. Like all debt instruments, a _____ entails the redistribution of financial assets over time, between the lender and the borrower.
  a. Loan0
  b. Thing
  c. Undefined
  d. Undefined

43. In business, particularly accounting, a _____ is the time intervals that the accounts, statement, payments, or other calculations cover.
  a. Thing
  b. Period0
  c. Undefined
  d. Undefined

44. A _____ is a method of using property as security for the payment of a debt.
  a. Mortgage0
  b. Thing
  c. Undefined
  d. Undefined

45. _____ is the income from capital investment paid in a series of regular payments.

Chapter 1. Functions, Graphs, and Models

a. Thing
b. Annuity0
c. Undefined
d. Undefined

46. _____ is a form of periodic payment from an employer to an employee, which is specified in an employment contract.
a. Thing
b. Gross pay0
c. Undefined
d. Undefined

47. A _____ is a form of periodic payment from an employer to an employee, which is specified in an employment contract.
a. Salary0
b. Thing
c. Undefined
d. Undefined

48. Multiple Signal Classification, also known as _____, is an algorithm used for frequency estimation and emitter location.
a. Music0
b. Thing
c. Undefined
d. Undefined

49. A _____ is a three-dimensional solid object bounded by six square faces, facets, or sides, with three meeting at each vertex.
a. Thing
b. Cube0
c. Undefined
d. Undefined

50. In mathematics, a _____ may be described informally as a number that can be given by an infinite decimal representation.

a. Thing
b. Real number0
c. Undefined
d. Undefined

51. In mathematics, the _____ of a function is the set of all "output" values produced by that function. Given a function $f : A \to B$, the _____ of f, is defined to be the set $\{x \in B : x = f(a) \text{ for some } a \in A\}$.
   a. Thing
   b. Range0
   c. Undefined
   d. Undefined

52. The _____ integers are all the integers from zero on upwards.
   a. Nonnegative0
   b. Thing
   c. Undefined
   d. Undefined

53. In plane geometry, a _____ is a polygon with four equal sides, four right angles, and parallel opposite sides. In algebra, the _____ of a number is that number multiplied by itself.
   a. Thing
   b. Square0
   c. Undefined
   d. Undefined

54. The _____ are the only integral domain whose positive elements are well-ordered, and in which order is preserved by addition. Like the natural numbers, the _____ form a countably infinite set. The set of all _____ is usually denoted in mathematics by a boldface Z .
   a. Thing
   b. Integers0
   c. Undefined
   d. Undefined

55. A _____ of a number is the product of that number with any integer.

a. Thing
b. Multiple0
c. Undefined
d. Undefined

56. In mathematics, a _____ of a number x is a number r such that r^2 = x, or in words, a number r whose square (the result of multiplying the number by itself) is x.
   a. Square root0
   b. Thing
   c. Undefined
   d. Undefined

57. In mathematics, a _____ of a complex-valued function f is a member x of the domain of f such that f(x) vanishes at x, that is, x : f (x) = 0.
   a. Thing
   b. Root0
   c. Undefined
   d. Undefined

58. A _____ is a number that is less than zero.
   a. Negative number0
   b. Thing
   c. Undefined
   d. Undefined

59. In mathematics, the _____ f is the collection of all ordered pairs . In particular, graph means the graphical representation of this collection, in the form of a curve or surface, together with axes, etc. Graphing on a Cartesian plane is sometimes referred to as curve sketching.
   a. Thing
   b. Graph of a function0
   c. Undefined
   d. Undefined

60. Acid _____ ratio measures the ability of a company to use its near cash or quick assets to immediately extinguish its current liabilities.

a. Test0
b. Thing
c. Undefined
d. Undefined

61. In linear algebra, the _____ of an n-by-n square matrix A is defined to be the sum of the elements on the main diagonal of A,
   a. Thing
   b. Trace0
   c. Undefined
   d. Undefined

62. A _____ defined function $f(x)$ of a real variable x is a function whose definition is given differently on disjoint subsets of its domain.
   a. Thing
   b. Piecewise0
   c. Undefined
   d. Undefined

63. In Euclidean geometry, a _____ is the set of all points in a plane at a fixed distance, called the radius, from a given point, the center.
   a. Thing
   b. Circle0
   c. Undefined
   d. Undefined

64. In mathematics, an inequality is a statement about the relative size or order of two objects. For example 14 > 10, or 14 is _____ 10.
   a. Thing
   b. Greater than0
   c. Undefined
   d. Undefined

65. _____ is a business term for the amount of money that a company receives from its activities in a given period, mostly from sales of products and/or services to customers

Chapter 1. Functions, Graphs, and Models

   a. Revenue0
   b. Thing
   c. Undefined
   d. Undefined

66. In mathematics, the multiplicative inverse of a number x, denoted 1/x or x^{-1}, is the number which, when multiplied by x, yields 1. The multiplicative inverse of x is also called the _____ of x.
   a. Thing
   b. Reciprocal0
   c. Undefined
   d. Undefined

67. In mathematics, an _____, mean, or central tendency of a data set refers to a measure of the "middle" or "expected" value of the data set.
   a. Average0
   b. Concept
   c. Undefined
   d. Undefined

68. Initial objects are also called _____, and terminal objects are also called final.
   a. Coterminal0
   b. Thing
   c. Undefined
   d. Undefined

69. A _____ are accounts maintained by commercial banks, savings and loan associations, credit unions, and mutual savings banks that pay interest but can not be used directly as money by, for example, writing a cheque.
   a. Thing
   b. Savings account0
   c. Undefined
   d. Undefined

70. _____ or investing is a term with several closely-related meanings in business management, finance and economics, related to saving or deferring consumption.

a. Investment0
b. Thing
c. Undefined
d. Undefined

71. In economics _____ means before deductions brutto, e.g. _____ domestic or national product, or _____ profit or income
  a. Thing
  b. Gross0
  c. Undefined
  d. Undefined

72. In mathematics, a matrix can be thought of as each row or _____ being a vector. Hence, a space formed by row vectors or _____ vectors are said to be a row space or a _____ space.
  a. Column0
  b. Concept
  c. Undefined
  d. Undefined

73. In elementary algebra, an _____ is a set that contains every real number between two indicated numbers and may contain the two numbers themselves.
  a. Interval0
  b. Thing
  c. Undefined
  d. Undefined

74. _____ is the notation in which permitted values for a variable are expressed as ranging over a certain interval; "5 < x < 9" is an example of the application of _____.
  a. Interval notation0
  b. Thing
  c. Undefined
  d. Undefined

75. A _____ is a one-dimensional picture in which the integers are shown as specially-marked points evenly spaced on a line.

Chapter 1. Functions, Graphs, and Models

a. Thing
b. Number line0
c. Undefined
d. Undefined

76. _____, either of the curved-bracket punctuation marks that together make a set of _____
a. Thing
b. Parentheses0
c. Undefined
d. Undefined

77. In mathematics, a _____ is a two-dimensional manifold or surface that is perfectly flat.
a. Plane0
b. Thing
c. Undefined
d. Undefined

78. Mathematical _____ are the wide variety of ways to capture an abstract mathematical concept or relationship.
a. Representations0
b. Thing
c. Undefined
d. Undefined

79. _____ is often used to describe the measurement of the steepness, incline, gradient, or grade of a straight line. The _____ is defined as the ratio of the "rise" divided by the "run" between two points on a line, or in other words, the ratio of the altitude change to the horizontal distance between any two points on the line.
a. Thing
b. Slope0
c. Undefined
d. Undefined

80. An _____ is when two lines intersect somewhere on a plane creating a right angle at intersection

Chapter 1. Functions, Graphs, and Models   17

   a. Thing
   b. Axes0
   c. Undefined
   d. Undefined

81. A _____ is a quantity that denotes the proportional amount or magnitude of one quantity relative to another.
   a. Thing
   b. Ratio0
   c. Undefined
   d. Undefined

82. In mathematics and logic, a _____ proof is a way of showing the truth or falsehood of a given statement by a straightforward combination of established facts, usually existing lemmas and theorems, without making any further assumptions.
   a. Thing
   b. Direct0
   c. Undefined
   d. Undefined

83. _____ is the relationship between two variables, like a ratio in which the two quantities being compared are different units.
   a. Direct variation0
   b. Thing
   c. Undefined
   d. Undefined

84. _____ is a special mathematical relationship between two quantities. Two quantities are called proportional if they vary in such a way that one of the quantities is a constant multiple of the other, or equivalently if they have a constant ratio.
   a. Thing
   b. Proportionality0
   c. Undefined
   d. Undefined

85. In mathematics and the mathematical sciences, a _____ is a fixed, but possibly unspecified, value. This is in contrast to a variable, which is not fixed.

a. Thing
b. Constant0
c. Undefined
d. Undefined

86. In mathematics, two quantities are called _____ if they vary in such a way that one of the quantities is a constant multiple of the other, or equivalently if they have a constant ratio.
a. Thing
b. Proportional0
c. Undefined
d. Undefined

87. Any point where a graph makes contact with an coordinate axis is called an _____ of the graph
a. Intercept0
b. Thing
c. Undefined
d. Undefined

88. A _____ is one of the basic shapes of geometry: a polygon with three vertices and three sides which are straight line segments.
a. Thing
b. Triangle0
c. Undefined
d. Undefined

89. In geometry, a _____ is a special kind of point, usually a corner of a polygon, polyhedron, or higher dimensional polytope. In the geometry of curves a _____ is a point of where the first derivative of curvature is zero. In graph theory, a _____ is the fundamental unit out of which graphs are formed
a. Vertex0
b. Thing
c. Undefined
d. Undefined

90. _____ is a way of expressing a number as a fraction of 100 per cent meaning "per hundred".

Chapter 1. Functions, Graphs, and Models

a. Percent0
b. Thing
c. Undefined
d. Undefined

91. In physics, _____ is an influence that may cause an object to accelerate. It may be experienced as a lift, a push, or a pull. The actual acceleration of the body is determined by the vector sum of all forces acting on it, known as net _____ or resultant _____.
a. Thing
b. Force0
c. Undefined
d. Undefined

92. Fixed costs are expenses whose total does not change in proportion to the activity of a business.Unit fixed costs decline with volume following a retangular hyperbola as the volume of production.Variable costs by contrast change in relation to the activity of a business such as sales or production volume.Along with variable costs,fixed costs make up one of the two components of total cost. In the most simple production function total cost is equal to fixed costs plus variable costs.In accounting terminology, fixed costs will broadly include all costs which are not included in cost of goods sold, and variable costs are those captured in costs of goods sold. The implicit assumption required to make the equivalence between the accounting and economics terminology is that the accounting period is equal to the period in which fixed costs do not vary in relation to production. In practice, this equivalence does not always hold and depending on the period under consideration by management, some overhead expenses can be adjusted by management, and the specific allocation of each expense to each category will be decided under cost accounting.In business planning and management accounting, usage of the terms fixed costs, variable costs and others will often differ from usage in economics, and may depend on the intended use. For example, costs may be segregated into per unit costs fixed costs per period, and variable costs as a proportion of revenue. Capital expenditures will usually be allocated separately, and depending on the purpose, a portion may be regularly allocated to expenses as depreciation and amortization and seen as a _____ per period, or the entire amount may be considered upfront fixed costs.
a. Fixed cost0
b. Thing
c. Undefined
d. Undefined

93. _____ are expenses whose total does not change in proportion to the activity of a business, within the relevant time period or scale of production

a. Fixed costs0
b. Thing
c. Undefined
d. Undefined

94. _____, from Latin meaning "to make progress", is defined in two different ways. Pure economic _____ is the increase in wealth that an investor has from making an investment, taking into consideration all costs associated with that investment including the opportunity cost of capital.
  a. Thing
  b. Profit0
  c. Undefined
  d. Undefined

95. _____ is a term that has several possible meanings all closely related to a firm's financial statements.
  a. Book value0
  b. Thing
  c. Undefined
  d. Undefined

96. _____ is a term used in accounting, economics and finance with reference to the fact that assets with finite lives lose value over time.
  a. Depreciation0
  b. Thing
  c. Undefined
  d. Undefined

97. _____ is a set, with some particular properties and usually some additional structure, such as the operations of addition or multiplication, for instance.
  a. Space0
  b. Thing
  c. Undefined
  d. Undefined

98. _____ are any documents that aim to streamline particular processes according to a set routine.

Chapter 1. Functions, Graphs, and Models

a. Guidelines0
b. Thing
c. Undefined
d. Undefined

99. _____ is the transport of people on a trip/journey or the process or time involved in a person or object moving from one location to another.
a. Travel0
b. Thing
c. Undefined
d. Undefined

100. In mathematics, a _____ function in the sense of algebraic geometry is an everywhere-defined, polynomial function on an algebraic variety V with values in the field K over which V is defined.
a. Regular0
b. Thing
c. Undefined
d. Undefined

101. _____ is a temperature scale named after the German physicist Daniel Gabriel _____ , who proposed it in 1724.
a. Fahrenheit0
b. Thing
c. Undefined
d. Undefined

102. In mathematics, there are several meanings of _____ depending on the subject.
a. Thing
b. Degree0
c. Undefined
d. Undefined

103. _____ is a physical property of a system that underlies the common notions of hot and cold; something that is hotter has the greater _____.

a. Thing
b. Temperature0
c. Undefined
d. Undefined

104. _____ is a unit of speed, expressing the number of international miles covered per hour.
a. Thing
b. Miles per hour0
c. Undefined
d. Undefined

105. _____ is a synonym for information.
a. Thing
b. Data0
c. Undefined
d. Undefined

106. In probability theory and statistics, a _____ is a number dividing the higher half of a sample, a population, or a probability distribution from the lower half.
a. Concept
b. Median0
c. Undefined
d. Undefined

107. _____ is the symbold used to indicate the nth root of a number
a. Thing
b. Radical0
c. Undefined
d. Undefined

108. In mathematics, a _____ number is a number which can be expressed as a ratio of two integers. Non-integer _____ numbers (commonly called fractions) are usually written as the vulgar fraction a / b, where b is not zero.

Chapter 1. Functions, Graphs, and Models

   a. Rational0
   b. Thing
   c. Undefined
   d. Undefined

109. _____ is a mathematical operation, written a^n, involving two numbers, the base a and the exponent n.
   a. Thing
   b. Exponentiating0
   c. Undefined
   d. Undefined

110. _____ is a mathematical operation, written a^n, involving two numbers, the base a and the exponent n.
   a. Thing
   b. Exponentiation0
   c. Undefined
   d. Undefined

111. An _____ is a combination of numbers, operators, grouping symbols and/or free variables and bound variables arranged in a meaningful way which can be evaluated..
   a. Expression0
   b. Thing
   c. Undefined
   d. Undefined

112. In mathematics, a _____ is any function which can be written as the ratio of two polynomial functions.
   a. Thing
   b. Rational function0
   c. Undefined
   d. Undefined

113. In economics, economic _____ is simply a state of the world where economic forces are balanced and in the absence of external influences the values of economic variables will not change.

a. Equilibrium0
b. Thing
c. Undefined
d. Undefined

114. In economics, supply and _____ describe market relations between prospective sellers and buyers of a good.
a. Thing
b. Demand0
c. Undefined
d. Undefined

115. _____ means "constancy", i.e. if something retains a certain feature even after we change a way of looking at it, then it is symmetric.
a. Thing
b. Symmetry0
c. Undefined
d. Undefined

116. A _____ is a negotiable instrument instructing a financial institution to pay a specific amount of a specific currency from a specific demand account held in the maker/depositor's name with that institution. Both the maker and payee may be natural persons or legal entities.
a. Check0
b. Thing
c. Undefined
d. Undefined

117. _____ is a set of numbers, in the broadest sense of the word, together with one or more operations, such as addition or multiplication.
a. Thing
b. Number system0
c. Undefined
d. Undefined

118. In mathematics, a _____ is a number in the form of a + bi where a and b are real numbers, and i is the imaginary unit, with the property $i^2 = -1$. The real number a is called the real part of the _____, and the real number b is the imaginary part.

a. Thing
b. Complex number0
c. Undefined
d. Undefined

119. In mathematics, a _____ is a polynomial equation of the second degree. The general form is $ax^2 + bx + c = 0$.
a. Thing
b. Quadratic equation0
c. Undefined
d. Undefined

120. A quadratic equation with real solutions, called roots, which may be real or complex, is given by the _____: $x = \frac{-b \pm \sqrt{b^2 - 4ac}}{2a}$.
a. Quadratic formula0
b. Thing
c. Undefined
d. Undefined

121. A _____ is a polynomial function of the form $f(x) = ax^2 + bx + c$, where a, b, c are real numbers and a , 0.
a. Event
b. Quadratic function0
c. Undefined
d. Undefined

122. _____ is a notation for writing numbers that is often used by scientists and mathematicians to make it easier to write large and small numbers.
a. Scientific notation0
b. Thing
c. Undefined
d. Undefined

123. In mathematics, a _____ is the result of multiplying, or an expression that identifies factors to be multiplied.

Chapter 1. Functions, Graphs, and Models

  a. Thing
  b. Product0
  c. Undefined
  d. Undefined

124. In mathematics, a _____ is a constant multiplicative factor of a certain object. The object can be such things as a variable, a vector, a function, etc. For example, the _____ of $9x^2$ is 9.
  a. Thing
  b. Coefficient0
  c. Undefined
  d. Undefined

125. In mathematics, the _____ of two sets A and B is the set that contains all elements of A that also belong to B (or equivalently, all elements of B that also belong to A), but no other elements.
  a. Thing
  b. Intersection0
  c. Undefined
  d. Undefined

126. In statistics, _____ means the most frequent value assumed by a random variable, or occurring in a sampling of a random variable.
  a. Mode0
  b. Concept
  c. Undefined
  d. Undefined

127. In geometry, a line _____ is a part of a line that is bounded by two end points, and contains every point on the line between its end points.
  a. Concept
  b. Segment0
  c. Undefined
  d. Undefined

128. A _____ is a part of a line that is bounded by two end points, and contains every point on the line between its end points.

a. Line segment0
b. Thing
c. Undefined
d. Undefined

129. _____ element of an element x with respect to a binary operation * with identity element e is an element y such that x * y = y * x = e. In particular,
a. Thing
b. Inverse0
c. Undefined
d. Undefined

130. The word _____ is used in a variety of ways in mathematics.
a. Thing
b. Index0
c. Undefined
d. Undefined

131. In mathematics, the _____ (or modulus) of a real number is its numerical value without regard to its sign.
a. Thing
b. Absolute value0
c. Undefined
d. Undefined

132. _____ has many meanings, most of which simply .
a. Power0
b. Thing
c. Undefined
d. Undefined

133. A _____ is an individual or household that purchases and uses goods and services generated within the economy.

a. Thing
b. Consumer0
c. Undefined
d. Undefined

134. _____ is the price at which the quantity demanded of a good or service is equal to the quantity supplied.
a. Equilibrium price0
b. Thing
c. Undefined
d. Undefined

135. In mathematics, a _____ number (or a _____) is a natural number that has exactly two (distinct) natural number divisors, which are 1 and the _____ number itself.
a. Thing
b. Prime0
c. Undefined
d. Undefined

136. _____ is the property of a physical object that quantifies the amount of matter and energy it is equivalent to.
a. Mass0
b. Thing
c. Undefined
d. Undefined

137. The metre (or _____, see spelling differences) is a measure of length. It is the basic unit of length in the metric system and in the International System of Units (SI), used around the world for general and scientific purposes.
a. Concept
b. Meter0
c. Undefined
d. Undefined

138. _____ is finding a curve which matches a series of data points and possibly other constraints.

Chapter 1. Functions, Graphs, and Models

a. Thing
b. Curve fitting0
c. Undefined
d. Undefined

139. A _____, scatter diagram or scatter graph is a graph used in statistics to visually display and relate two quantitative variables of a multidimensional data set by displaying the data as a collection of points, each having one coordinate on a horizontal and one on a vertical axis.
a. Thing
b. Scatterplot0
c. Undefined
d. Undefined

140. _____ is a regression method that models the relationship between a dependent variable Y, independent variables Xp, and a random term å.
a. Thing
b. Linear regression0
c. Undefined
d. Undefined

141. A _____ is the quantity that defines certain relatively constant characteristics of systems or functions..
a. Thing
b. Parameter0
c. Undefined
d. Undefined

142. In geometry, the _____ of an object is a point in some sense in the middle of the object.
a. Thing
b. Center0
c. Undefined
d. Undefined

143. In mathematics and elsewhere, the adjective _____ means fourth order, such as the function x4. A _____ number is a number which equals the fourth power of an integer.

Chapter 1. Functions, Graphs, and Models

a. Quartic0
b. Thing
c. Undefined
d. Undefined

144. A _____ is a polynomial function with a degree of four. It has the same limit when the argument goes to positive or negative infinity.
a. Quartic function0
b. Thing
c. Undefined
d. Undefined

145. _____ is a function of the form
a. Thing
b. Cubic function0
c. Undefined
d. Undefined

146. _____ is a mathematical science pertaining to the collection, analysis, interpretation or explanation, and presentation of data. It is applicable to a wide variety of academic disciplines, from the physical and social sciences to the humanities.
a. Statistics0
b. Thing
c. Undefined
d. Undefined

147. _____ is the level of functional and/or metabolic efficiency of an organism at both the micro level.
a. Thing
b. Health0
c. Undefined
d. Undefined

148. A frame of _____ is a particular perspective from which the universe is observed.

a. Thing
b. Reference0
c. Undefined
d. Undefined

149. In mathematics, a _____ is a rectangular table of numbers or, more generally, a table consisting of abstract quantities that can be added and multiplied.
a. Matrix0
b. Thing
c. Undefined
d. Undefined

150. _____ are a measure of time.
a. Thing
b. Minutes0
c. Undefined
d. Undefined

151. In a company, _____ is the sum of all financial records of salaries, wages, bonuses, and deductions.
a. Thing
b. Payroll0
c. Undefined
d. Undefined

1. In mathematics, a _____ is the result of multiplying, or an expression that identifies factors to be multiplied.
   a. Product0
   b. Thing
   c. Undefined
   d. Undefined

2. In calculus, the _____ is a formula for the derivative of the composite of two functions.
   a. Chain rule0
   b. Concept
   c. Undefined
   d. Undefined

3. In mathematics, a _____ is the end result of a division problem. It can also be expressed as the number of times the divisor divides into the dividend.
   a. Quotient0
   b. Thing
   c. Undefined
   d. Undefined

4. The _____ is a method of finding the derivative of a function that is the quotient of two other functions for which derivatives exist.
   a. Quotient rule0
   b. Thing
   c. Undefined
   d. Undefined

5. A _____ is a special kind of ratio, indicating a relationship between two measurements with different units, such as miles to gallons or cents to pounds.
   a. Thing
   b. Rate0
   c. Undefined
   d. Undefined

6. A _____ is the result of the addition of a set of numbers. The numbers may be natural numbers, complex numbers, matrices, or still more complicated objects. An infinite _____ is a subtle procedure known as a series.

Chapter 2. Differentiation

a. Sum0
b. Thing
c. Undefined
d. Undefined

7. In mathematics, an _____, mean, or central tendency of a data set refers to a measure of the "middle" or "expected" value of the data set.
a. Average0
b. Concept
c. Undefined
d. Undefined

8. _____ has many meanings, most of which simply .
a. Thing
b. Power0
c. Undefined
d. Undefined

9. The _____ is a measurement of how a function changes when the values of its inputs change.
a. Thing
b. Derivative0
c. Undefined
d. Undefined

10. The function difference divided by the point difference is known as the _____
a. Difference quotient0
b. Thing
c. Undefined
d. Undefined

11. _____, a field in mathematics, is the study of how functions change when their inputs change. The primary object of study in _____ is the derivative.

a. Differential calculus0
b. Thing
c. Undefined
d. Undefined

12. In trigonometry, the _____ is a function defined as $\tan x = \sin x / \cos x$. The function is so-named because it can be defined as the length of a certain segment of a _____ (in the geometric sense) to the unit circle. In plane geometry, a line is _____ to a curve, at some point, if both line and curve pass through the point with the same direction.
   a. Tangent0
   b. Thing
   c. Undefined
   d. Undefined

13. The mathematical concept of a _____ expresses the intuitive idea of deterministic dependence between two quantities, one of which is viewed as primary and the other as secondary. A _____ then is a way to associate a unique output for each input of a specified type, for example, a real number or an element of a given set.
   a. Thing
   b. Function0
   c. Undefined
   d. Undefined

14. In linear algebra, the _____ of an n-by-n square matrix A is defined to be the sum of the elements on the main diagonal of A,
   a. Trace0
   b. Thing
   c. Undefined
   d. Undefined

15. In geographic information systems, a _____ comprises an entity with a geographic location, typically determined by points, arcs, or polygons. Carriageways and cadastres exemplify _____ data.
   a. Thing
   b. Feature0
   c. Undefined
   d. Undefined

16. A _____ defined function f(x) of a real variable x is a function whose definition is given differently on disjoint subsets of its domain.
   a. Thing
   b. Piecewise0
   c. Undefined
   d. Undefined

17. The _____ is a fundamental concept in analysis. Informally, a function f can be made as close to L as desired, by making x close enough to p.
   a. Limit of a function0
   b. Thing
   c. Undefined
   d. Undefined

18. A _____ function is a function for which, intuitively, small changes in the input result in small changes in the output.
   a. Event
   b. Continuous0
   c. Undefined
   d. Undefined

19. _____ are the basic objects of study in graph theory. Informally speaking, a graph is a set of objects called points, nodes, or vertices connected by links called lines or edges.
   a. Thing
   b. Graphs0
   c. Undefined
   d. Undefined

20. In mathematics, a _____ of a k-place relation $L \subseteq X_1 \times ... \times X_k$ is one of the sets X_j, $1 \leq j \leq k$. In the special case where k = 2 and $L \subseteq X_1 \times X_2$ is a function $L : X_1 \to X_2$, it is conventional to refer to X_1 as the _____ of the function and to refer to X_2 as the codomain of the function.
   a. Thing
   b. Domain0
   c. Undefined
   d. Undefined

21. Mathematical _____ is used to represent ideas.
   a. Thing
   b. Notation0
   c. Undefined
   d. Undefined

22. In elementary algebra, an _____ is a set that contains every real number between two indicated numbers and may contain the two numbers themselves.
   a. Thing
   b. Interval0
   c. Undefined
   d. Undefined

23. A _____ is a function for which, intuitively, small changes in the input result in small changes in the output.
   a. Event
   b. Continuous function0
   c. Undefined
   d. Undefined

24. In mathematics and the mathematical sciences, a _____ is a fixed, but possibly unspecified, value. This is in contrast to a variable, which is not fixed.
   a. Constant0
   b. Thing
   c. Undefined
   d. Undefined

25. _____ is a function whose values do not vary and thus are constant.
   a. Constant function0
   b. Thing
   c. Undefined
   d. Undefined

26. In mathematics, science including computer science, linguistics and engineering, an _____ is, generally speaking, an independent variable or input to a function.

Chapter 2. Differentiation

a. Thing
b. Argument0
c. Undefined
d. Undefined

27. The word _____ comes from the Latin word linearis, which means created by lines.
a. Linear0
b. Thing
c. Undefined
d. Undefined

28. A _____ is a first degree polynomial mathematical function of the form: f(x) = mx + b where m and b are real constants and x is a real variable.
a. Thing
b. Linear function0
c. Undefined
d. Undefined

29. In mathematics, a _____ is an expression that is constructed from one or more variables and constants, using only the operations of addition, subtraction, multiplication, and constant positive whole number exponents. is a _____. Note in particular that division by an expression containing a variable is not in general allowed in polynomials. [1]
a. Polynomial0
b. Thing
c. Undefined
d. Undefined

30. In common philosophical language, a proposition or _____, is the content of an assertion, that is, it is true-or-false and defined by the meaning of a particular piece of language.
a. Statement0
b. Concept
c. Undefined
d. Undefined

31. _____ is the transport of people on a trip/journey or the process or time involved in a person or object moving from one location to another.

a. Travel0
b. Thing
c. Undefined
d. Undefined

32. A _____ is a unit of length, usually used to measure distance, in a number of different systems, including Imperial units, United States customary units and Norwegian/Swedish mil. Its size can vary from system to system, but in each is between 1 and 10 kilometers. In contemporary English contexts _____ refers to either:
   a. Mile0
   b. Thing
   c. Undefined
   d. Undefined

33. In sociology and biology a _____ is the collection of people or organisms of a particular species living in a given geographic area or space, usually measured by a census.
   a. Thing
   b. Population0
   c. Undefined
   d. Undefined

34. _____ is change in population over time, and can be quantified as the change in the number of individuals in a population per unit time.
   a. Thing
   b. Population growth0
   c. Undefined
   d. Undefined

35. A _____ signifies a point or points of probability on a subject e.g., the _____ of creativity, which allows for the formation of rule or norm or law by interpretation of the phenomena events that can be created.
   a. Principle0
   b. Thing
   c. Undefined
   d. Undefined

36. The _____ integers are all the integers from zero on upwards.

a. Nonnegative0
b. Thing
c. Undefined
d. Undefined

37. A _____ is a symbolic representation denoting a quantity or expression. It often represents an "unknown" quantity that has the potential to change.
a. Thing
b. Variable0
c. Undefined
d. Undefined

38. An _____ is a combination of numbers, operators, grouping symbols and/or free variables and bound variables arranged in a meaningful way which can be evaluated..
a. Thing
b. Expression0
c. Undefined
d. Undefined

39. In mathematics, the concept of a _____ tries to capture the intuitive idea of a geometrical one-dimensional and continuous object. A simple example is the circle.
a. Curve0
b. Thing
c. Undefined
d. Undefined

40. In mathematics, _____ are the intuitive idea of a geometrical one-dimensional and continuous object.
a. Curves0
b. Thing
c. Undefined
d. Undefined

41. A _____ is a quantity that denotes the proportional amount or magnitude of one quantity relative to another.

a. Thing
b. Ratio0
c. Undefined
d. Undefined

42. _____ is often used to describe the measurement of the steepness, incline, gradient, or grade of a straight line. The _____ is defined as the ratio of the "rise" divided by the "run" between two points on a line, or in other words, the ratio of the altitude change to the horizontal distance between any two points on the line.
a. Slope0
b. Thing
c. Undefined
d. Undefined

43. _____ is a trigonometric function that is the reciprocal of cosine.
a. Thing
b. Secant0
c. Undefined
d. Undefined

44. _____ of a curve is a line that intersects two or more points on the curve.
a. Secant line0
b. Thing
c. Undefined
d. Undefined

45. A _____ is the part of a fraction that tells how many equal parts make up a whole, and which is used in the name of the fraction: "halves", "thirds", "fourths" or "quarters", "fifths" and so on.
a. Concept
b. Denominator0
c. Undefined
d. Undefined

46. The _____ of measurement are a globally standardized and modernized form of the metric system.

a. Units0
b. Thing
c. Undefined
d. Undefined

47. A _____ is an individual or household that purchases and uses goods and services generated within the economy.
a. Consumer0
b. Thing
c. Undefined
d. Undefined

48. _____ is a kind of property which exists as magnitude or multitude. It is among the basic classes of things along with quality, substance, change, and relation.
a. Thing
b. Amount0
c. Undefined
d. Undefined

49. _____ is a business term for the amount of money that a company receives from its activities in a given period, mostly from sales of products and/or services to customers
a. Revenue0
b. Thing
c. Undefined
d. Undefined

50. In mathematics, a matrix can be thought of as each row or _____ being a vector. Hence, a space formed by row vectors or _____ vectors are said to be a row space or a _____ space.
a. Concept
b. Column0
c. Undefined
d. Undefined

51. In probability theory and statistics, a _____ is a number dividing the higher half of a sample, a population, or a probability distribution from the lower half.

a. Concept
b. Median0
c. Undefined
d. Undefined

52. In geometry, the _____ of an object is a point in some sense in the middle of the object.
a. Thing
b. Center0
c. Undefined
d. Undefined

53. _____ is a mathematical science pertaining to the collection, analysis, interpretation or explanation, and presentation of data. It is applicable to a wide variety of academic disciplines, from the physical and social sciences to the humanities.
a. Thing
b. Statistics0
c. Undefined
d. Undefined

54. _____ is the level of functional and/or metabolic efficiency of an organism at both the micro level.
a. Thing
b. Health0
c. Undefined
d. Undefined

55. The word _____ is used in a variety of ways in mathematics.
a. Thing
b. Index0
c. Undefined
d. Undefined

56. A _____ number is a positive integer which has a positive divisor other than one or itself.

Chapter 2. Differentiation 43

 a. Thing
 b. Composite0
 c. Undefined
 d. Undefined

57. In mathematics, the _____ f is the collection of all ordered pairs . In particular, graph means the graphical representation of this collection, in the form of a curve or surface, together with axes, etc. Graphing on a Cartesian plane is sometimes referred to as curve sketching.
 a. Thing
 b. Graph of a function0
 c. Undefined
 d. Undefined

58. _____ has two distinct but etymologically-related meanings: one in geometry and one in trigonometry.
 a. Tangent line0
 b. Thing
 c. Undefined
 d. Undefined

59. In Euclidean geometry, a _____ is the set of all points in a plane at a fixed distance, called the radius, from a given point, the center.
 a. Thing
 b. Circle0
 c. Undefined
 d. Undefined

60. A _____ is a set of numbers that designate location in a given reference system, such as x,y in a planar _____ system or an x,y,z in a three-dimensional _____ system.
 a. Coordinate0
 b. Thing
 c. Undefined
 d. Undefined

61. A _____ is a negotiable instrument instructing a financial institution to pay a specific amount of a specific currency from a specific demand account held in the maker/depositor's name with that institution. Both the maker and payee may be natural persons or legal entities.

a. Check0
b. Thing
c. Undefined
d. Undefined

62. In mathematics, a _____ may be described informally as a number that can be given by an infinite decimal representation.
a. Thing
b. Real number0
c. Undefined
d. Undefined

63. In mathematics, defined and _____ are used to explain whether or not expressions have meaningful, sensible, and unambiguous values.
a. Undefined0
b. Thing
c. Undefined
d. Undefined

64. _____ is a technique of numerical analysis to produce an estimate of the derivative of a mathematical function or function subroutine using values from the function and perhaps other knowledge about the function.
a. Thing
b. Numerical differentiation0
c. Undefined
d. Undefined

65. _____ or investing is a term with several closely-related meanings in business management, finance and economics, related to saving or deferring consumption.
a. Investment0
b. Thing
c. Undefined
d. Undefined

66. The _____, the average in everyday English, which is also called the arithmetic _____ (and is distinguished from the geometric _____ or harmonic _____). The average is also called the sample _____. The expected value of a random variable, which is also called the population _____.

a. Mean0
b. Thing
c. Undefined
d. Undefined

67. _____ is a mathematical subject that includes the study of limits, derivatives, integrals, and power series and constitutes a major part of modern university curriculum.
   a. Calculus0
   b. Thing
   c. Undefined
   d. Undefined

68. _____ is a method for differentiating expressions involving exponentiation the power operation.
   a. Thing
   b. Power rule0
   c. Undefined
   d. Undefined

69. In mathematics, a _____ number is a number which can be expressed as a ratio of two integers. Non-integer _____ numbers (commonly called fractions) are usually written as the vulgar fraction a / b, where b is not zero.
   a. Thing
   b. Rational0
   c. Undefined
   d. Undefined

70. In mathematics, a _____ is a demonstration that, assuming certain axioms, some statement is necessarily true.
   a. Thing
   b. Proof0
   c. Undefined
   d. Undefined

71. In mathematics, a _____ is a statement that can be proved on the basis of explicitly stated or previously agreed assumptions.

a. Thing
b. Theorem0
c. Undefined
d. Undefined

72. In calculus, the _____ in differentiation is a method of finding the derivative of a function that is the sum of two other functions for which derivatives exist.
   a. Sum Rule0
   b. Thing
   c. Undefined
   d. Undefined

73. In astronomy, geography, geometry and related sciences and contexts, a plane is said to be _____ at a given point if it is locally perpendicular to the gradient of the gravity field, i.e., with the direction of the gravitational force at that point.
   a. Thing
   b. Horizontal0
   c. Undefined
   d. Undefined

74. In mathematics, a _____ is a polynomial equation of the second degree. The general form is $ax^2 + bx + c = 0$.
   a. Quadratic equation0
   b. Thing
   c. Undefined
   d. Undefined

75. A quadratic equation with real solutions, called roots, which may be real or complex, is given by the _____: $x = \frac{-b \pm \sqrt{b^2 - 4ac}}{2a}$.
   a. Quadratic formula0
   b. Thing
   c. Undefined
   d. Undefined

76. _____ is the largest positive integer that divides both numbers without remainder.

Chapter 2. Differentiation   47

   a. Thing
   b. Common Factor0
   c. Undefined
   d. Undefined

77. Sir Isaac _____, was an English physicist, mathematician, astronomer, natural philosopher, and alchemist, regarded by many as the greatest figure in the history of science
   a. Person
   b. Newton0
   c. Undefined
   d. Undefined

78. _____ was a German mathematician and philosopher. He invented calculus independently of Newton, and his notation is the one in general use since.
   a. Leibniz0
   b. Person
   c. Undefined
   d. Undefined

79. _____ of an object is its speed in a particular direction.
   a. Velocity0
   b. Thing
   c. Undefined
   d. Undefined

80. _____ is defined as the rate of change or derivative with respect to time of velocity.
   a. Acceleration0
   b. Thing
   c. Undefined
   d. Undefined

81. U.S. liquid _____ is legally defined as 231 cubic inches, and is equal to 3.785411784 litres or abotu 0.13368 cubic feet. This is the most common definition of a _____. The U.S. fluid ounce is defined as 1/128 of a U.S. _____.

a. Gallon0
b. Thing
c. Undefined
d. Undefined

82. The _____ of a solid object is the three-dimensional concept of how much space it occupies, often quantified numerically.
a. Thing
b. Volume0
c. Undefined
d. Undefined

83. In classical geometry, a _____ of a circle or sphere is any line segment from its center to its boundary. By extension, the _____ of a circle or sphere is the length of any such segment. The _____ is half the diameter. In science and engineering the term _____ of curvature is commonly used as a synonym for _____.
a. Thing
b. Radius0
c. Undefined
d. Undefined

84. A _____ is 360° or 2δ radians.
a. Turn0
b. Thing
c. Undefined
d. Undefined

85. Initial objects are also called _____, and terminal objects are also called final.
a. Thing
b. Coterminal0
c. Undefined
d. Undefined

86. _____, from Latin meaning "to make progress", is defined in two different ways. Pure economic _____ is the increase in wealth that an investor has from making an investment, taking into consideration all costs associated with that investment including the opportunity cost of capital.

Chapter 2. Differentiation

a. Thing
b. Profit0
c. Undefined
d. Undefined

87. _____ is the change in total cost that arises when the quantity produced changes by one unit.
a. Marginal cost0
b. Thing
c. Undefined
d. Undefined

88. In mathematics a _____ is a function which defines a distance between elements of a set.
a. Metric0
b. Thing
c. Undefined
d. Undefined

89. In economics, supply and _____ describe market relations between prospective sellers and buyers of a good.
a. Thing
b. Demand0
c. Undefined
d. Undefined

90. In mathematics, a _____ function in the sense of algebraic geometry is an everywhere-defined, polynomial function on an algebraic variety V with values in the field K over which V is defined.
a. Regular0
b. Thing
c. Undefined
d. Undefined

91. _____ is a temperature scale named after the German physicist Daniel Gabriel _____ , who proposed it in 1724.

a. Fahrenheit0
b. Thing
c. Undefined
d. Undefined

92. In mathematics, there are several meanings of _____ depending on the subject.
a. Thing
b. Degree0
c. Undefined
d. Undefined

93. _____ is a physical property of a system that underlies the common notions of hot and cold; something that is hotter has the greater _____.
a. Temperature0
b. Thing
c. Undefined
d. Undefined

94. The _____ is the distance around a closed curve. _____ is a kind of perimeter.
a. Circumference0
b. Thing
c. Undefined
d. Undefined

95. In plane geometry, a _____ is a polygon with four equal sides, four right angles, and parallel opposite sides. In algebra, the _____ of a number is that number multiplied by itself.
a. Square0
b. Thing
c. Undefined
d. Undefined

96. _____ the expected value of a random variable displays the average or central value of the variable. It is a summary value of the distribution of the variable.

a. Determining0
b. Thing
c. Undefined
d. Undefined

97. In mathematics, the _____ of a function is the set of all "output" values produced by that function. Given a function $f: A \to B$, the _____ of f, is defined to be the set $\{x \in B : x = f(a) \text{ for some } a \in A\}$.
   a. Thing
   b. Range0
   c. Undefined
   d. Undefined

98. The _____ governs the differentiation of products of differentiable functions.
   a. Product rule0
   b. Thing
   c. Undefined
   d. Undefined

99. A _____ is a numeral used to indicate a count. The most common use of the word today is to name the part of a fraction that tells the number or count of equal parts.
   a. Thing
   b. Numerator0
   c. Undefined
   d. Undefined

100. The plus and _____ signs are mathematical symbols used to represent the notions of positive and negative as well as the operations of addition and subtraction.
   a. Thing
   b. Minus0
   c. Undefined
   d. Undefined

101. _____ is the extra revenue that an additional unit of product will bring a firm. It can also be described as the change in total revenue/change in number of units sold.

a. Thing
b. Marginal revenue0
c. Undefined
d. Undefined

102. In economics _____ means before deductions brutto, e.g. _____ domestic or national product, or _____ profit or income
a. Thing
b. Gross0
c. Undefined
d. Undefined

103. An _____ of a product of sums expresses it as a sum of products by using the fact that multiplication distributes over addition.
a. Expansion0
b. Thing
c. Undefined
d. Undefined

104. In mathematics, a _____ is a mathematical statement which appears likely to be true, but has not been formally proven to be true under the rules of mathematical logic.
a. Conjecture0
b. Concept
c. Undefined
d. Undefined

105. In mathematics, a _____ of a positive integer n is a way of writing n as a sum of positive integers.
a. Composition0
b. Thing
c. Undefined
d. Undefined

106. Equivalence is the condition of being _____ or essentially equal.

Chapter 2. Differentiation

   a. Equivalent0
   b. Thing
   c. Undefined
   d. Undefined

107. _____ is the fee paid on borrowed money.
   a. Interest0
   b. Thing
   c. Undefined
   d. Undefined

108. _____ interest refers to the fact that whenever interest is calculated, it is based not only on the original principal, but also on any unpaid interest that has been added to the principal.
   a. Compound0
   b. Thing
   c. Undefined
   d. Undefined

109. _____ refers to the fact that whenever interest is calculated, it is based not only on the original principal, but also on any unpaid interest that has been added to the principal. The more frequently interest is compounded, the faster the balance grows.
   a. Compound interest0
   b. Concept
   c. Undefined
   d. Undefined

110. An _____ is the fee paid on borrow money.
   a. Interest rate0
   b. Concept
   c. Undefined
   d. Undefined

111. A _____ is the quantity that defines certain relatively constant characteristics of systems or functions..

Chapter 2. Differentiation

a. Parameter0
b. Thing
c. Undefined
d. Undefined

112. _____ is a mathematical operation, written a^n, involving two numbers, the base a and the exponent n.
a. Exponentiating0
b. Thing
c. Undefined
d. Undefined

113. _____ is a mathematical operation, written a^n, involving two numbers, the base a and the exponent n.
a. Thing
b. Exponentiation0
c. Undefined
d. Undefined

114. Acid _____ ratio measures the ability of a company to use its near cash or quick assets to immediately extinguish its current liabilities.
a. Test0
b. Thing
c. Undefined
d. Undefined

115. A frame of _____ is a particular perspective from which the universe is observed.
a. Thing
b. Reference0
c. Undefined
d. Undefined

116. In the scientific method, an _____ (Latin: ex-+-periri, "of (or from) trying"), is a set of actions and observations, performed in the context of solving a particular problem or question, in order to support or falsify a hypothesis or research concerning phenomena.

Chapter 2. Differentiation

a. Thing
b. Experiment0
c. Undefined
d. Undefined

117. _____ are a measure of time.
a. Minutes0
b. Thing
c. Undefined
d. Undefined

118. In mathematics, the _____ is a conic section generated by the intersection of a right circular conical surface and a plane parallel to a generating straight line of that surface. It can also be defined as locus of points in a plane which are equidistant from a given point.
a. Thing
b. Parabola0
c. Undefined
d. Undefined

119. _____ is a synonym for information.
a. Thing
b. Data0
c. Undefined
d. Undefined

120. _____ is finding a curve which matches a series of data points and possibly other constraints.
a. Curve fitting0
b. Thing
c. Undefined
d. Undefined

121. In mathematics, a _____ of a complex-valued function f is a member x of the domain of f such that f(x) vanishes at x, that is, x : f (x) = 0.

a. Root0
b. Thing
c. Undefined
d. Undefined

122. In geometry, a line _____ is a part of a line that is bounded by two end points, and contains every point on the line between its end points.
   a. Concept
   b. Segment0
   c. Undefined
   d. Undefined

123. A _____ is a part of a line that is bounded by two end points, and contains every point on the line between its end points.
   a. Line segment0
   b. Thing
   c. Undefined
   d. Undefined

124. In mathematics and elsewhere, the adjective _____ means fourth order, such as the function x4. A _____ number is a number which equals the fourth power of an integer.
   a. Quartic0
   b. Thing
   c. Undefined
   d. Undefined

125. A _____ is a statement or claimt that a particular event will occur in the future in more certain terms than a forecast.
   a. Thing
   b. Prediction0
   c. Undefined
   d. Undefined

126. _____ is the path a moving object follows through space.

a. Thing
b. Projectile motion0
c. Undefined
d. Undefined

Chapter 3. Applications of Differentiation

1. _____ are the basic objects of study in graph theory. Informally speaking, a graph is a set of objects called points, nodes, or vertices connected by links called lines or edges.
   a. Thing
   b. Graphs0
   c. Undefined
   d. Undefined

2. A _____ is a special kind of ratio, indicating a relationship between two measurements with different units, such as miles to gallons or cents to pounds.
   a. Thing
   b. Rate0
   c. Undefined
   d. Undefined

3. In mathematics, a _____ number is a number which can be expressed as a ratio of two integers. Non-integer _____ numbers (commonly called fractions) are usually written as the vulgar fraction a / b, where b is not zero.
   a. Thing
   b. Rational0
   c. Undefined
   d. Undefined

4. In mathematics, a _____ is any function which can be written as the ratio of two polynomial functions.
   a. Rational function0
   b. Thing
   c. Undefined
   d. Undefined

5. An _____ is a straight line or curve A to which another curve B approaches closer and closer as one moves along it. As one moves along B, the space between it and the _____ A becomes smaller and smaller, and can in fact be made as small as one could wish by going far enough along. A curve may or may not touch or cross its _____. In fact, the curve may intersect the _____ an infinite number of times.
   a. Thing
   b. Asymptote0
   c. Undefined
   d. Undefined

6. _____ is to give an equation R(x,y) = S(x,y) that at least in part has the same graph as y = f(x).

Chapter 3. Applications of Differentiation

a. Implicit differentiation0
b. Thing
c. Undefined
d. Undefined

7. In differential calculus, _____ problems involve finding the rate at which a quantity is changing by relating that quantity to other quantities whose rates of change are known.
   a. Thing
   b. Related rates0
   c. Undefined
   d. Undefined

8. The _____ is a measurement of how a function changes when the values of its inputs change.
   a. Thing
   b. Derivative0
   c. Undefined
   d. Undefined

9. A _____ is traditionally an infinitesimally small change in a variable.
   a. Differential0
   b. Thing
   c. Undefined
   d. Undefined

10. _____, a field in mathematics, is the study of how functions change when their inputs change. The primary object of study in _____ is the derivative.
    a. Differential calculus0
    b. Thing
    c. Undefined
    d. Undefined

11. The mathematical concept of a _____ expresses the intuitive idea of deterministic dependence between two quantities, one of which is viewed as primary and the other as secondary. A _____ then is a way to associate a unique output for each input of a specified type, for example, a real number or an element of a given set.

a. Function0
b. Thing
c. Undefined
d. Undefined

12. In mathematics, a _____ is the result of multiplying, or an expression that identifies factors to be multiplied.
a. Product0
b. Thing
c. Undefined
d. Undefined

13. In mathematics, a subset of Euclidean space R^n is called _____ if it is closed and bounded.
a. Compact0
b. Thing
c. Undefined
d. Undefined

14. In linear algebra, the _____ of an n-by-n square matrix A is defined to be the sum of the elements on the main diagonal of A,
a. Trace0
b. Thing
c. Undefined
d. Undefined

15. In mathematics, the _____ f is the collection of all ordered pairs . In particular, graph means the graphical representation of this collection, in the form of a curve or surface, together with axes, etc. Graphing on a Cartesian plane is sometimes referred to as curve sketching.
a. Graph of a function0
b. Thing
c. Undefined
d. Undefined

16. In geographic information systems, a _____ comprises an entity with a geographic location, typically determined by points, arcs, or polygons. Carriageways and cadastres exemplify _____ data.

Chapter 3. Applications of Differentiation

a. Feature0
b. Thing
c. Undefined
d. Undefined

17. In elementary algebra, an _____ is a set that contains every real number between two indicated numbers and may contain the two numbers themselves.
a. Thing
b. Interval0
c. Undefined
d. Undefined

18. _____ is often used to describe the measurement of the steepness, incline, gradient, or grade of a straight line. The _____ is defined as the ratio of the "rise" divided by the "run" between two points on a line, or in other words, the ratio of the altitude change to the horizontal distance between any two points on the line.
a. Thing
b. Slope0
c. Undefined
d. Undefined

19. The word _____ comes from the Latin word linearis, which means created by lines.
a. Linear0
b. Thing
c. Undefined
d. Undefined

20. A _____ is a first degree polynomial mathematical function of the form: f(x) = mx + b where m and b are real constants and x is a real variable.
a. Thing
b. Linear function0
c. Undefined
d. Undefined

21. In trigonometry, the _____ is a function defined as tan x = $\sin x / \cos x$. The function is so-named because it can be defined as the length of a certain segment of a _____ (in the geometric sense) to the unit circle. In plane geometry, a line is _____ to a curve, at some point, if both line and curve pass through the point with the same direction.

a. Tangent0
b. Thing
c. Undefined
d. Undefined

22. _____ has two distinct but etymologically-related meanings: one in geometry and one in trigonometry.
a. Tangent line0
b. Thing
c. Undefined
d. Undefined

23. _____ is a point on the domain of a function
a. Critical point0
b. Thing
c. Undefined
d. Undefined

24. In astronomy, geography, geometry and related sciences and contexts, a plane is said to be _____ at a given point if it is locally perpendicular to the gradient of the gravity field, i.e., with the direction of the gravitational force at that point.
a. Horizontal0
b. Thing
c. Undefined
d. Undefined

25. In mathematics, a _____ of a k-place relation $L \subseteq X_1 \times \ldots \times X_k$ is one of the sets X_j, $1 \leq j \leq k$. In the special case where k = 2 and $L \subseteq X_1 \times X_2$ is a function $L : X_1 \to X_2$, it is conventional to refer to X_1 as the _____ of the function and to refer to X_2 as the codomain of the function.
a. Domain0
b. Thing
c. Undefined
d. Undefined

26. The _____ is the lowest point in a certain portion of a graph.

a. Thing
b. Relative minimum0
c. Undefined
d. Undefined

27. A _____ function is a function for which, intuitively, small changes in the input result in small changes in the output.
a. Event
b. Continuous0
c. Undefined
d. Undefined

28. in mathematics, maxima and minima, known collectively as _____, are the largest value maximum or smallest value minimum, that a function takes in a point either within a given neighborhood or on the function domain in its entirety global extremum.
a. Extrema0
b. Thing
c. Undefined
d. Undefined

29. The term _____ refers to the largest and the smallest element of a set.
a. Thing
b. Extreme value0
c. Undefined
d. Undefined

30. In mathematics, a _____ is a statement that can be proved on the basis of explicitly stated or previously agreed assumptions.
a. Theorem0
b. Thing
c. Undefined
d. Undefined

31. The _____ is the highest point in a certain portion of a graph.

a. Thing
b. Relative maximum0
c. Undefined
d. Undefined

32. Acid _____ ratio measures the ability of a company to use its near cash or quick assets to immediately extinguish its current liabilities.
   a. Test0
   b. Thing
   c. Undefined
   d. Undefined

33. A _____ signifies a point or points of probability on a subject e.g., the _____ of creativity, which allows for the formation of rule or norm or law by interpretation of the phenomena events that can be created.
   a. Thing
   b. Principle0
   c. Undefined
   d. Undefined

34. A frame of _____ is a particular perspective from which the universe is observed.
   a. Reference0
   b. Thing
   c. Undefined
   d. Undefined

35. In mathematics, the concept of a _____ tries to capture the intuitive idea of a geometrical one-dimensional and continuous object. A simple example is the circle.
   a. Curve0
   b. Thing
   c. Undefined
   d. Undefined

36. In mathematics, a _____ may be described informally as a number that can be given by an infinite decimal representation.

Chapter 3. Applications of Differentiation

a. Real number0
b. Thing
c. Undefined
d. Undefined

37. The _____ of measurement are a globally standardized and modernized form of the metric system.
a. Units0
b. Thing
c. Undefined
d. Undefined

38. _____ is a physical property of a system that underlies the common notions of hot and cold; something that is hotter has the greater _____.
a. Temperature0
b. Thing
c. Undefined
d. Undefined

39. _____ algebra (sometimes called General algebra) is the field of mathematics that studies the ideas common to all algebraic structures.
a. Universal0
b. Thing
c. Undefined
d. Undefined

40. In geometry, the _____ of an object is a point in some sense in the middle of the object.
a. Thing
b. Center0
c. Undefined
d. Undefined

41. _____, usually denoted symbolically by the Greek letter phi, Î¦, gives the location of a place on Earth north or south of the equator. _____ is an angular measurement in degrees (marked with Â°) ranging from 0Â° at the Equator (low _____) to 90Â° at the poles (90Â° N for the North Pole or 90Â° S for the South Pole; high _____). The complementary angle of a _____ is called the colatitude.

a. Thing
b. Latitude0
c. Undefined
d. Undefined

42. _____ describes the location of a place on Earth east or west of a north-south line called the Prime Meridian.
a. Longitude0
b. Thing
c. Undefined
d. Undefined

43. In mathematics, there are several meanings of _____ depending on the subject.
a. Thing
b. Degree0
c. Undefined
d. Undefined

44. A _____ is a negotiable instrument instructing a financial institution to pay a specific amount of a specific currency from a specific demand account held in the maker/depositor's name with that institution. Both the maker and payee may be natural persons or legal entities.
a. Check0
b. Thing
c. Undefined
d. Undefined

45. _____ is a statistical measure of the average length of survival of a living thing.
a. Thing
b. Life expectancy0
c. Undefined
d. Undefined

46. _____ is a function of the form

Chapter 3. Applications of Differentiation

a. Cubic function0
b. Thing
c. Undefined
d. Undefined

47. _____ is a synonym for information.
   a. Data0
   b. Thing
   c. Undefined
   d. Undefined

48. A _____ is an instrument used in geometry technical drawing and engineering/building to measure distances and/or to rule straight lines.
   a. Ruler0
   b. Thing
   c. Undefined
   d. Undefined

49. The word _____ means curving in or hollowed inward.
   a. Thing
   b. Concavity0
   c. Undefined
   d. Undefined

50. In mathematics, maxima and minima, known collectively as extrema, are the largest value maximum or smallest value minimum, that a function takes in a point either within a given neighborhood local _____ or on the function domain in its entirety global _____.
   a. Extremum0
   b. Thing
   c. Undefined
   d. Undefined

51. The _____, the average in everyday English, which is also called the arithmetic _____ (and is distinguished from the geometric _____ or harmonic _____). The average is also called the sample _____. The expected value of a random variable, which is also called the population _____.

a. Mean0
b. Thing
c. Undefined
d. Undefined

52. _____ is a a point on a curve at which the tangent crosses the curve itself.
a. Thing
b. Inflection point0
c. Undefined
d. Undefined

53. _____ is a free computer algebra system based on a 1982 version of Macsyma
a. Maxima0
b. Thing
c. Undefined
d. Undefined

54. _____ are points in the domain of a function at which the function takes a largest value or smallest value, either within a given neighborhood or on the function domain in its entirety.
a. Maxima and minima0
b. Thing
c. Undefined
d. Undefined

55. In mathematics, maxima and _____, known collectively as extrema, are points in the domain of a function at which the function takes a largest value .
a. Minima0
b. Thing
c. Undefined
d. Undefined

56. _____, from Latin meaning "to make progress", is defined in two different ways. Pure economic _____ is the increase in wealth that an investor has from making an investment, taking into consideration all costs associated with that investment including the opportunity cost of capital.

a. Profit0
b. Thing
c. Undefined
d. Undefined

57. _____ is a business term for the amount of money that a company receives from its activities in a given period, mostly from sales of products and/or services to customers
a. Revenue0
b. Thing
c. Undefined
d. Undefined

58. An _____ is when two lines intersect somewhere on a plane creating a right angle at intersection
a. Thing
b. Axes0
c. Undefined
d. Undefined

59. In physics, _____ is an influence that may cause an object to accelerate. It may be experienced as a lift, a push, or a pull. The actual acceleration of the body is determined by the vector sum of all forces acting on it, known as net _____ or resultant _____.
a. Force0
b. Thing
c. Undefined
d. Undefined

60. _____ of an object is its speed in a particular direction.
a. Velocity0
b. Thing
c. Undefined
d. Undefined

61. In classical geometry, a _____ of a circle or sphere is any line segment from its center to its boundary. By extension, the _____ of a circle or sphere is the length of any such segment. The _____ is half the diameter. In science and engineering the term _____ of curvature is commonly used as a synonym for _____.

a. Radius0
b. Thing
c. Undefined
d. Undefined

62. In mathematics and the mathematical sciences, a _____ is a fixed, but possibly unspecified, value. This is in contrast to a variable, which is not fixed.
a. Thing
b. Constant0
c. Undefined
d. Undefined

63. In mathematics, an _____, mean, or central tendency of a data set refers to a measure of the "middle" or "expected" value of the data set.
a. Concept
b. Average0
c. Undefined
d. Undefined

64. _____ is a temperature scale named after the German physicist Daniel Gabriel _____ , who proposed it in 1724.
a. Fahrenheit0
b. Thing
c. Undefined
d. Undefined

65. In mathematics and elsewhere, the adjective _____ means fourth order, such as the function x4. A _____ number is a number which equals the fourth power of an integer.
a. Quartic0
b. Thing
c. Undefined
d. Undefined

66. A _____ is a polynomial function with a degree of four. It has the same limit when the argument goes to positive or negative infinity.

a. Thing
b. Quartic function0
c. Undefined
d. Undefined

67. In mathematics, a _____ is a rectangular table of numbers or, more generally, a table consisting of abstract quantities that can be added and multiplied.
   a. Matrix0
   b. Thing
   c. Undefined
   d. Undefined

68. The metre (or _____, see spelling differences) is a measure of length. It is the basic unit of length in the metric system and in the International System of Units (SI), used around the world for general and scientific purposes.
   a. Meter0
   b. Concept
   c. Undefined
   d. Undefined

69. _____ are a measure of time.
   a. Minutes0
   b. Thing
   c. Undefined
   d. Undefined

70. _____ is the state of being greater than any finite number, however large.
   a. Thing
   b. Infinity0
   c. Undefined
   d. Undefined

71. In mathematics, a _____ is an expression that is constructed from one or more variables and constants, using only the operations of addition, subtraction, multiplication, and constant positive whole number exponents. is a _____. Note in particular that division by an expression containing a variable is not in general allowed in polynomials. [1]

Chapter 3. Applications of Differentiation

a. Thing
b. Polynomial0
c. Undefined
d. Undefined

72. A _____ is a set of numbers that designate location in a given reference system, such as x,y in a planar _____ system or an x,y,z in a three-dimensional _____ system.
   a. Thing
   b. Coordinate0
   c. Undefined
   d. Undefined

73. A _____ is a numeral used to indicate a count. The most common use of the word today is to name the part of a fraction that tells the number or count of equal parts.
   a. Numerator0
   b. Thing
   c. Undefined
   d. Undefined

74. _____ is a branch of mathematics concerning the study of structure, relation and quantity.
   a. Algebra0
   b. Concept
   c. Undefined
   d. Undefined

75. _____ is a kind of property which exists as magnitude or multitude. It is among the basic classes of things along with quality, substance, change, and relation.
   a. Amount0
   b. Thing
   c. Undefined
   d. Undefined

76. A _____ is the part of a fraction that tells how many equal parts make up a whole, and which is used in the name of the fraction: "halves", "thirds", "fourths" or "quarters", "fifths" and so on.

Chapter 3. Applications of Differentiation

a. Denominator0
b. Concept
c. Undefined
d. Undefined

77. In statistics, _____ means the most frequent value assumed by a random variable, or occurring in a sampling of a random variable.
a. Concept
b. Mode0
c. Undefined
d. Undefined

78. _____ has many meanings, most of which simply .
a. Power0
b. Thing
c. Undefined
d. Undefined

79. The _____ is the maximum of the degrees of all terms in the polynomial.
a. Degree of a polynomial0
b. Thing
c. Undefined
d. Undefined

80. _____ is a straight line or curve A to which another curve B the one being studied approaches closer and closer as one moves along it.
a. Thing
b. Vertical asymptote0
c. Undefined
d. Undefined

81. _____ is the largest positive integer that divides both numbers without remainder.

Chapter 3. Applications of Differentiation

   a. Thing
   b. Common Factor0
   c. Undefined
   d. Undefined

82. An _____ is a combination of numbers, operators, grouping symbols and/or free variables and bound variables arranged in a meaningful way which can be evaluated..
   a. Thing
   b. Expression0
   c. Undefined
   d. Undefined

83. In geometry, an _____ angle is an angle that is not a 90 degree angle, or an angle that is divisible by 90: 180, 270, 360/0
   a. Thing
   b. Oblique0
   c. Undefined
   d. Undefined

84. In mathematics, a _____ is a constant multiplicative factor of a certain object. The object can be such things as a variable, a vector, a function, etc. For example, the _____ of $9x^2$ is 9.
   a. Coefficient0
   b. Thing
   c. Undefined
   d. Undefined

85. In mathematics, a _____ is the end result of a division problem. It can also be expressed as the number of times the divisor divides into the dividend.
   a. Thing
   b. Quotient0
   c. Undefined
   d. Undefined

86. A _____ is the part of the dividend that is left over when the dividend is not evenly divisible by the divisor.

a. Remainder0
b. Thing
c. Undefined
d. Undefined

87. Any point where a graph makes contact with an coordinate axis is called an _____ of the graph
a. Intercept0
b. Thing
c. Undefined
d. Undefined

88. In geometry, an _____ is a point at which a line segment or ray terminates.
a. Thing
b. Endpoint0
c. Undefined
d. Undefined

89. In mathematics, defined and _____ are used to explain whether or not expressions have meaningful, sensible, and unambiguous values.
a. Undefined0
b. Thing
c. Undefined
d. Undefined

90. In mathematics, an inequality is a statement about the relative size or order of two objects. For example 14 > 10, or 14 is _____ 10.
a. Thing
b. Greater than0
c. Undefined
d. Undefined

91. Initial objects are also called _____, and terminal objects are also called final.

Chapter 3. Applications of Differentiation

a. Thing
b. Coterminal0
c. Undefined
d. Undefined

92. _____ is the fee paid on borrowed money.
a. Interest0
b. Thing
c. Undefined
d. Undefined

93. Deductive _____ is the kind of _____ in which the conclusion is necessitated by, or reached from, previously known facts (the premises).
a. Thing
b. Reasoning0
c. Undefined
d. Undefined

94. In mathematics, _____ are the intuitive idea of a geometrical one-dimensional and continuous object.
a. Curves0
b. Thing
c. Undefined
d. Undefined

95. The _____ of a solid object is the three-dimensional concept of how much space it occupies, often quantified numerically.
a. Volume0
b. Thing
c. Undefined
d. Undefined

96. In mathematics, in the field of group theory, a _____ of a group is a quasisimple subnormal subgroup.

Chapter 3. Applications of Differentiation 77

a. Component0
b. Concept
c. Undefined
d. Undefined

97. _____ is a mathematical subject that includes the study of limits, derivatives, integrals, and power series and constitutes a major part of modern university curriculum.
a. Thing
b. Calculus0
c. Undefined
d. Undefined

98. A _____ is a symbolic representation denoting a quantity or expression. It often represents an "unknown" quantity that has the potential to change.
a. Thing
b. Variable0
c. Undefined
d. Undefined

99. A _____ is the result of the addition of a set of numbers. The numbers may be natural numbers, complex numbers, matrices, or still more complicated objects. An infinite _____ is a subtle procedure known as a series.
a. Sum0
b. Thing
c. Undefined
d. Undefined

100. In plane geometry, a _____ is a polygon with four equal sides, four right angles, and parallel opposite sides. In algebra, the _____ of a number is that number multiplied by itself.
a. Thing
b. Square0
c. Undefined
d. Undefined

101. _____ is the use of marginal concepts within economics. Marginal concepts include marginal cost, marginal productivity and marginal utility, the law of diminishing rates of substitution, and the law of diminishing marginal utility.

a. Marginal analysis0
b. Thing
c. Undefined
d. Undefined

102. A _____ is a number that is less than zero.
a. Thing
b. Negative number0
c. Undefined
d. Undefined

103. _____ is the change in total cost that arises when the quantity produced changes by one unit.
a. Thing
b. Marginal cost0
c. Undefined
d. Undefined

104. _____ is the extra revenue that an additional unit of product will bring a firm. It can also be described as the change in total revenue/change in number of units sold.
a. Thing
b. Marginal revenue0
c. Undefined
d. Undefined

105. _____ the expected value of a random variable displays the average or central value of the variable. It is a summary value of the distribution of the variable.
a. Determining0
b. Thing
c. Undefined
d. Undefined

106. _____ is a list of goods and materials, or those goods and materials themselves, held available in stock by a business

Chapter 3. Applications of Differentiation

a. Thing
b. Inventory0
c. Undefined
d. Undefined

107. Order theory is a branch of mathematics that studies various kinds of binary relations that capture the intuitive notion of a mathematical _____.
a. Ordering0
b. Thing
c. Undefined
d. Undefined

108. In banking and accountancy, the outstanding _____ is the amount of money owned, or due, that remains in a deposit account or a loan account at a given date, after all past remittances, payments and withdrawal have been accounted for.
a. Balance0
b. Thing
c. Undefined
d. Undefined

109. In business, particularly accounting, a _____ is the time intervals that the accounts, statement, payments, or other calculations cover.
a. Period0
b. Thing
c. Undefined
d. Undefined

Chapter 3. Applications of Differentiation

110. Fixed costs are expenses whose total does not change in proportion to the activity of a business.Unit fixed costs decline with volume following a retangular hyperbola as the volume of production.Variable costs by contrast change in relation to the activity of a business such as sales or production volume.Along with variable costs,fixed costs make up one of the two components of total cost. In the most simple production function total cost is equal to fixed costs plus variable costs.In accounting terminology, fixed costs will broadly include all costs which are not included in cost of goods sold, and variable costs are those captured in costs of goods sold. The implicit assumption required to make the equivalence between the accounting and economics terminology is that the accounting period is equal to the period in which fixed costs do not vary in relation to production. In practice, this equivalence does not always hold and depending on the period under consideration by management, some overhead expenses can be adjusted by management, and the specific allocation of each expense to each category will be decided under cost accounting.In business planning and management accounting, usage of the terms fixed costs, variable costs and others will often differ from usage in economics, and may depend on the intended use. For example, costs may be segregated into per unit costs fixed costs per period, and variable costs as a proportion of revenue. Capital expenditures will usually be allocated separately, and depending on the purpose, a portion may be regularly allocated to expenses as depreciation and amortization and seen as a _____ per period, or the entire amount may be considered upfront fixed costs.
   a. Thing
   b. Fixed cost0
   c. Undefined
   d. Undefined

111. The act of _____ is the calculated approximation of a result which is usable even if input data may be incomplete, uncertain, or noisy.
   a. Thing
   b. Estimating0
   c. Undefined
   d. Undefined

112. _____ is the distance around a given two-dimensional object. As a general rule, the _____ of a polygon can always be calculated by adding all the length of the sides together. So, the formula for triangles is P = a + b + c, where a, b and c stand for each side of it. For quadrilaterals the equation is P = a + b + c + d. For equilateral polygons, P = na, where n is the number of sides and a is the side length.
   a. Perimeter0
   b. Thing
   c. Undefined
   d. Undefined

113. In geometry, a _____ is defined as a quadrilateral where all four of its angles are right angles.

Chapter 3. Applications of Differentiation

a. Rectangle0
b. Thing
c. Undefined
d. Undefined

114. In economics, supply and _____ describe market relations between prospective sellers and buyers of a good.
a. Thing
b. Demand0
c. Undefined
d. Undefined

115. In topology and related areas of mathematics a _____ or Moore-Smith sequence is a generalization of a sequence, intended to unify the various notions of limit and generalize them to arbitrary topological spaces.
a. Thing
b. Net0
c. Undefined
d. Undefined

116. _____ is an economics theory, that refers to individuals or societies gaining the maximum amount out of the resources they have available to them.
a. Maximization0
b. Thing
c. Undefined
d. Undefined

117. A _____ is a plan of action to guide decisions and actions.
a. Thing
b. Policy0
c. Undefined
d. Undefined

118. In sociology and biology a _____ is the collection of people or organisms of a particular species living in a given geographic area or space, usually measured by a census.

Chapter 3. Applications of Differentiation

a. Population0
b. Thing
c. Undefined
d. Undefined

119. In mathematics, two quantities are called _____ if they vary in such a way that one of the quantities is a constant multiple of the other, or equivalently if they have a constant ratio.

a. Thing
b. Proportional0
c. Undefined
d. Undefined

120. A _____ are accounts maintained by commercial banks, savings and loan associations, credit unions, and mutual savings banks that pay interest but can not be used directly as money by, for example, writing a cheque.

a. Thing
b. Savings account0
c. Undefined
d. Undefined

121. An _____ is the fee paid on borrow money.

a. Interest rate0
b. Concept
c. Undefined
d. Undefined

122. A _____ is a function that assigns a number to subsets of a given set.

a. Thing
b. Measure0
c. Undefined
d. Undefined

123. In Euclidean geometry, a _____ is the set of all points in a plane at a fixed distance, called the radius, from a given point, the center.

Chapter 3. Applications of Differentiation

a. Circle0
b. Thing
c. Undefined
d. Undefined

124. A _____ is a unit of length, usually used to measure distance, in a number of different systems, including Imperial units, United States customary units and Norwegian/Swedish mil. Its size can vary from system to system, but in each is between 1 and 10 kilometers. In contemporary English contexts _____ refers to either:
  a. Mile0
  b. Thing
  c. Undefined
  d. Undefined

125. In mathematics, the additive inverse, or _____ of a number n is the number that, when added to n, yields zero. The additive inverse of n is denoted −n. For example, 7 is −7, because 7 + (−7) = 0, and the additive inverse of −0.3 is 0.3, because −0.3 + 0.3 = 0.
  a. Opposite0
  b. Thing
  c. Undefined
  d. Undefined

126. In mathematics, the _____ of a number n is the number that, when added to n, yields zero. The _____ of n is denoted −n. For example, 7 is −7, because 7 + (−7) = 0, and the _____ of −0.3 is 0.3, because −0.3 + 0.3 = 0.
  a. Additive inverse0
  b. Thing
  c. Undefined
  d. Undefined

127. Mathematical _____ is used to represent ideas.
  a. Thing
  b. Notation0
  c. Undefined
  d. Undefined

128. The function difference divided by the point difference is known as the _____

Chapter 3. Applications of Differentiation

a. Thing
b. Difference quotient0
c. Undefined
d. Undefined

129. A _____ is a number, figure, or indicator that appears below the normal line of type, typically used in a formula, mathematical expression, or description of a chemical compound.
a. Subscript0
b. Thing
c. Undefined
d. Undefined

130. _____ was a German mathematician and philosopher. He invented calculus independently of Newton, and his notation is the one in general use since.
a. Leibniz0
b. Person
c. Undefined
d. Undefined

131. _____ named in honor of the 17th century German philosopher and mathematician Gottfried Wilhelm Leibniz, was originally the use of expressions such as dx and dy and to represent "infinitely small" or infinitesimal increments of quantities x and y, just as Äx and Äy represent finite increments of x and y respectively.
a. Thing
b. Leibniz notation0
c. Undefined
d. Undefined

132. A _____ is a statement or claimt that a particular event will occur in the future in more certain terms than a forecast.
a. Thing
b. Prediction0
c. Undefined
d. Undefined

133. The term _____ can refer to an integer which is the square of some other integer, or an algebraic expression that can be factored as the square of some other expression.

Chapter 3. Applications of Differentiation

a. Perfect square0
b. Thing
c. Undefined
d. Undefined

134. The _____ governs the differentiation of products of differentiable functions.
a. Product rule0
b. Thing
c. Undefined
d. Undefined

135. In mathematics, _____ expressions is used to reduce the expression into the lowest possible term.
a. Simplifying0
b. Thing
c. Undefined
d. Undefined

136. _____ is a method for differentiating expressions involving exponentiation the power operation.
a. Power rule0
b. Thing
c. Undefined
d. Undefined

137. _____ is the transport of people on a trip/journey or the process or time involved in a person or object moving from one location to another.
a. Travel0
b. Thing
c. Undefined
d. Undefined

138. In mathematics, a matrix can be thought of as each row or _____ being a vector. Hence, a space formed by row vectors or _____ vectors are said to be a row space or a _____ space.

a. Concept
b. Column0
c. Undefined
d. Undefined

Chapter 4. Exponential and Logarithmic Functions

1. _____ is the fee paid on borrowed money.
    a. Thing
    b. Interest0
    c. Undefined
    d. Undefined

2. In sociology and biology a _____ is the collection of people or organisms of a particular species living in a given geographic area or space, usually measured by a census.
    a. Thing
    b. Population0
    c. Undefined
    d. Undefined

3. _____ is change in population over time, and can be quantified as the change in the number of individuals in a population per unit time.
    a. Thing
    b. Population growth0
    c. Undefined
    d. Undefined

4. In economics and business studies, the _____ is an elasticity that measures the nature and degree of the relationship between changes in quantity demanded of a good and changes in its price.
    a. Thing
    b. Elasticity of demand0
    c. Undefined
    d. Undefined

5. In mathematics, _____ growth occurs when the growth rate of a function is always proportional to the function's current size.
    a. Exponential0
    b. Thing
    c. Undefined
    d. Undefined

6. _____ is one of the most important functions in mathematics. A function commonly used to study growth and decay

a. Exponential function0
b. Thing
c. Undefined
d. Undefined

7. In economics, supply and _____ describe market relations between prospective sellers and buyers of a good.
   a. Thing
   b. Demand0
   c. Undefined
   d. Undefined

8. The _____ is a measurement of how a function changes when the values of its inputs change.
   a. Thing
   b. Derivative0
   c. Undefined
   d. Undefined

9. The mathematical concept of a _____ expresses the intuitive idea of deterministic dependence between two quantities, one of which is viewed as primary and the other as secondary. A _____ then is a way to associate a unique output for each input of a specified type, for example, a real number or an element of a given set.
   a. Function0
   b. Thing
   c. Undefined
   d. Undefined

10. In mathematics, a _____ number is a number which can be expressed as a ratio of two integers. Non-integer _____ numbers (commonly called fractions) are usually written as the vulgar fraction a / b, where b is not zero.
    a. Thing
    b. Rational0
    c. Undefined
    d. Undefined

11. The _____ is the total number of human beings alive on the planet Earth at a given time.

Chapter 4. Exponential and Logarithmic Functions

a. World population0
b. Thing
c. Undefined
d. Undefined

12. An _____ is a combination of numbers, operators, grouping symbols and/or free variables and bound variables arranged in a meaningful way which can be evaluated..
   a. Thing
   b. Expression0
   c. Undefined
   d. Undefined

13. _____ is the state of being greater than any finite real or natural number, however large.
   a. Thing
   b. Infinite0
   c. Undefined
   d. Undefined

14. In mathematics, an _____ number is any real number that is not a rational number- that is, it is a number which cannot be expressed as a fraction m/n, where m and n are integers.
   a. Irrational0
   b. Thing
   c. Undefined
   d. Undefined

15. In mathematics, an _____ is any real number that is not a rational number ¡ª that is, it is a number which cannot be expressed as m/n, where m and n are integers.
   a. Irrational number0
   b. Thing
   c. Undefined
   d. Undefined

16. In mathematics, a _____ may be described informally as a number that can be given by an infinite decimal representation.

Chapter 4. Exponential and Logarithmic Functions

a. Real number0
b. Thing
c. Undefined
d. Undefined

17. A _____ function is a function for which, intuitively, small changes in the input result in small changes in the output.
a. Event
b. Continuous0
c. Undefined
d. Undefined

18. A _____ is a symbolic representation denoting a quantity or expression. It often represents an "unknown" quantity that has the potential to change.
a. Thing
b. Variable0
c. Undefined
d. Undefined

19. In mathematics and the mathematical sciences, a _____ is a fixed, but possibly unspecified, value. This is in contrast to a variable, which is not fixed.
a. Thing
b. Constant0
c. Undefined
d. Undefined

20. Initial objects are also called _____, and terminal objects are also called final.
a. Thing
b. Coterminal0
c. Undefined
d. Undefined

21. A _____ is a special kind of ratio, indicating a relationship between two measurements with different units, such as miles to gallons or cents to pounds.

Chapter 4. Exponential and Logarithmic Functions

a. Rate0
b. Thing
c. Undefined
d. Undefined

22. _____ is a kind of property which exists as magnitude or multitude. It is among the basic classes of things along with quality, substance, change, and relation.
a. Thing
b. Amount0
c. Undefined
d. Undefined

23. _____ interest refers to the fact that whenever interest is calculated, it is based not only on the original principal, but also on any unpaid interest that has been added to the principal.
a. Thing
b. Compound0
c. Undefined
d. Undefined

24. _____ refers to the fact that whenever interest is calculated, it is based not only on the original principal, but also on any unpaid interest that has been added to the principal. The more frequently interest is compounded, the faster the balance grows.
a. Concept
b. Compound interest0
c. Undefined
d. Undefined

25. An _____ is the fee paid on borrow money.
a. Interest rate0
b. Concept
c. Undefined
d. Undefined

26. _____ or investing is a term with several closely-related meanings in business management, finance and economics, related to saving or deferring consumption.

Chapter 4. Exponential and Logarithmic Functions

    a. Thing
    b. Investment0
    c. Undefined
    d. Undefined

27. In linear algebra, the _____ of an n-by-n square matrix A is defined to be the sum of the elements on the main diagonal of A,
    a. Thing
    b. Trace0
    c. Undefined
    d. Undefined

28. _____ are the basic objects of study in graph theory. Informally speaking, a graph is a set of objects called points, nodes, or vertices connected by links called lines or edges.
    a. Thing
    b. Graphs0
    c. Undefined
    d. Undefined

29. _____ is often used to describe the measurement of the steepness, incline, gradient, or grade of a straight line. The _____ is defined as the ratio of the "rise" divided by the "run" between two points on a line, or in other words, the ratio of the altitude change to the horizontal distance between any two points on the line.
    a. Slope0
    b. Thing
    c. Undefined
    d. Undefined

30. In trigonometry, the _____ is a function defined as $\tan x = \sin x / \cos x$. The function is so-named because it can be defined as the length of a certain segment of a _____ (in the geometric sense) to the unit circle. In plane geometry, a line is _____ to a curve, at some point, if both line and curve pass through the point with the same direction.
    a. Tangent0
    b. Thing
    c. Undefined
    d. Undefined

31. _____ has two distinct but etymologically-related meanings: one in geometry and one in trigonometry.

a. Thing
b. Tangent line0
c. Undefined
d. Undefined

32. In mathematics, a _____ is a statement that can be proved on the basis of explicitly stated or previously agreed assumptions.
a. Thing
b. Theorem0
c. Undefined
d. Undefined

33. _____ has many meanings, most of which simply .
a. Thing
b. Power0
c. Undefined
d. Undefined

34. _____ is a mathematical subject that includes the study of limits, derivatives, integrals, and power series and constitutes a major part of modern university curriculum.
a. Calculus0
b. Thing
c. Undefined
d. Undefined

35. _____ is a point on the domain of a function
a. Critical point0
b. Thing
c. Undefined
d. Undefined

36. _____ is a a point on a curve at which the tangent crosses the curve itself.

a. Thing
b. Inflection point0
c. Undefined
d. Undefined

37. The _____ integers are all the integers from zero on upwards.
   a. Nonnegative0
   b. Thing
   c. Undefined
   d. Undefined

38. _____ is a business term for the amount of money that a company receives from its activities in a given period, mostly from sales of products and/or services to customers
   a. Revenue0
   b. Thing
   c. Undefined
   d. Undefined

39. In physics, a _____ may refer to the scalar _____ or to the vector _____.
   a. Thing
   b. Potential0
   c. Undefined
   d. Undefined

40. A _____ is a plan of action to guide decisions and actions.
   a. Policy0
   b. Thing
   c. Undefined
   d. Undefined

41. Equivalence is the condition of being _____ or essentially equal.

Chapter 4. Exponential and Logarithmic Functions

a. Equivalent0
b. Thing
c. Undefined
d. Undefined

42. _____ is the logarithm to the base e, where e is an irrational constant approximately equal to 2.718281828459.
a. Thing
b. Natural logarithm0
c. Undefined
d. Undefined

43. In mathematics, a _____ of a number x is the exponent y of the power by such that $x = b^y$. The value used for the base b must be neither 0 nor 1, nor a root of 1 in the case of the extension to complex numbers, and is typically 10, e, or 2.
a. Logarithm0
b. Thing
c. Undefined
d. Undefined

44. _____ element of an element x with respect to a binary operation * with identity element e is an element y such that x * y = y * x = e. In particular,
a. Thing
b. Inverse0
c. Undefined
d. Undefined

45. In mathematics, a _____ is a demonstration that, assuming certain axioms, some statement is necessarily true.
a. Thing
b. Proof0
c. Undefined
d. Undefined

46. _____ is a mathematical operation, written a^n, involving two numbers, the base a and the exponent n.

Chapter 4. Exponential and Logarithmic Functions

a. Thing
b. Exponentiating0
c. Undefined
d. Undefined

47. _____ is a mathematical operation, written a^n, involving two numbers, the base a and the exponent n.
a. Exponentiation0
b. Thing
c. Undefined
d. Undefined

48. In mathematics, the _____ is the logarithm with base 10.
a. Thing
b. Common logarithm0
c. Undefined
d. Undefined

49. An _____ is when two lines intersect somewhere on a plane creating a right angle at intersection
a. Thing
b. Axes0
c. Undefined
d. Undefined

50. Mathematical _____ is used to represent ideas.
a. Thing
b. Notation0
c. Undefined
d. Undefined

51. _____ is a set, with some particular properties and usually some additional structure, such as the operations of addition or multiplication, for instance.

a. Space0
b. Thing
c. Undefined
d. Undefined

52. The deductive-nomological model is a formalized view of scientific _____ in natural language.
   a. Explanation0
   b. Thing
   c. Undefined
   d. Undefined

53. _____ is the process of reducing the number of significant digits in a number.
   a. Rounding0
   b. Concept
   c. Undefined
   d. Undefined

54. In geographic information systems, a _____ comprises an entity with a geographic location, typically determined by points, arcs, or polygons. Carriageways and cadastres exemplify _____ data.
   a. Thing
   b. Feature0
   c. Undefined
   d. Undefined

55. An _____ is a collection of two not necessarily distinct objects, one of which is distinguished as the first coordinate and the other as the second coordinate.
   a. Thing
   b. Ordered pair0
   c. Undefined
   d. Undefined

56. In mathematics, the _____ of a function is the set of all "output" values produced by that function. Given a function $f: A \to B$, the _____ of f, is defined to be the set $\{x \in B : x = f(a) \text{ for some } a \in A\}$.

Chapter 4. Exponential and Logarithmic Functions

   a. Range0
   b. Thing
   c. Undefined
   d. Undefined

57. In mathematics, a _____ of a k-place relation $L \subseteq X_1 \times ... \times X_k$ is one of the sets X_j, $1 \leq j \leq k$. In the special case where k = 2 and $L \subseteq X_1 \times X_2$ is a function $L : X_1 \to X_2$, it is conventional to refer to X_1 as the _____ of the function and to refer to X_2 as the codomain of the function.
   a. Thing
   b. Domain0
   c. Undefined
   d. Undefined

58. In the scientific method, an _____ (Latin: ex-+-periri, "of (or from) trying"), is a set of actions and observations, performed in the context of solving a particular problem or question, in order to support or falsify a hypothesis or research concerning phenomena.
   a. Experiment0
   b. Thing
   c. Undefined
   d. Undefined

59. In mathematics, a _____ is the result of multiplying, or an expression that identifies factors to be multiplied.
   a. Product0
   b. Thing
   c. Undefined
   d. Undefined

60. _____, from Latin meaning "to make progress", is defined in two different ways. Pure economic _____ is the increase in wealth that an investor has from making an investment, taking into consideration all costs associated with that investment including the opportunity cost of capital.
   a. Thing
   b. Profit0
   c. Undefined
   d. Undefined

61. The _____ of measurement are a globally standardized and modernized form of the metric system.

a. Units0
b. Thing
c. Undefined
d. Undefined

62. In business, particularly accounting, a _____ is the time intervals that the accounts, statement, payments, or other calculations cover.
a. Thing
b. Period0
c. Undefined
d. Undefined

63. In mathematics, an _____, mean, or central tendency of a data set refers to a measure of the "middle" or "expected" value of the data set.
a. Concept
b. Average0
c. Undefined
d. Undefined

64. The _____ is the period of time required for a quantity to double in size or value.
a. Thing
b. Doubling time0
c. Undefined
d. Undefined

65. In mathematics, _____ occurs when the growth rate of a function is always proportional to the function's current size.
a. Thing
b. Exponential growth0
c. Undefined
d. Undefined

66. In mathematics, _____ are essentially word problems that are designed to use mathematical critical thinking in everyday situations.

Chapter 4. Exponential and Logarithmic Functions

   a. Application problems0
   b. Thing
   c. Undefined
   d. Undefined

67. A _____ is traditionally an infinitesimally small change in a variable.
   a. Differential0
   b. Thing
   c. Undefined
   d. Undefined

68. A _____ is a mathematical equation for an unknown function of one or several variables which relates the values of the function itself and of its derivatives of various orders.
   a. Thing
   b. Differential equation0
   c. Undefined
   d. Undefined

69. _____ over a given field is a polynomial with coefficients in that field.
   a. Algebraic equation0
   b. Thing
   c. Undefined
   d. Undefined

70. In mathematics, two quantities are called _____ if they vary in such a way that one of the quantities is a constant multiple of the other, or equivalently if they have a constant ratio.
   a. Proportional0
   b. Thing
   c. Undefined
   d. Undefined

71. In mathematics, factorization (British English: factorisation) or factoring is the decomposition of an object (for example, a number, a polynomial, or a matrix) into a product of other objects, or _____, which when multiplied together give the original.

Chapter 4. Exponential and Logarithmic Functions 101

a. Thing
b. Factors0
c. Undefined
d. Undefined

72. The _____, the average in everyday English, which is also called the arithmetic _____ (and is distinguished from the geometric _____ or harmonic _____). The average is also called the sample _____. The expected value of a random variable, which is also called the population _____.
   a. Thing
   b. Mean0
   c. Undefined
   d. Undefined

73. In banking and accountancy, the outstanding _____ is the amount of money owned, or due, that remains in a deposit account or a loan account at a given date, after all past remittances, payments and withdrawal have been accounted for.
   a. Thing
   b. Balance0
   c. Undefined
   d. Undefined

74. A _____ is a function that assigns a number to subsets of a given set.
   a. Thing
   b. Measure0
   c. Undefined
   d. Undefined

75. A _____ is a unit of length, usually used to measure distance, in a number of different systems, including Imperial units, United States customary units and Norwegian/Swedish mil. Its size can vary from system to system, but in each is between 1 and 10 kilometers. In contemporary English contexts _____ refers to either:
   a. Thing
   b. Mile0
   c. Undefined
   d. Undefined

76. A _____ is a deliberate process for transforming one or more inputs into one or more results.

a. Calculation0
b. Thing
c. Undefined
d. Undefined

77. A _____ is 360° or 2δ radians.
a. Thing
b. Turn0
c. Undefined
d. Undefined

78. The population _____ is the total number of human beings alive on the planet Earth at a given time.
a. Thing
b. Of the world0
c. Undefined
d. Undefined

79. _____ is a synonym for information.
a. Thing
b. Data0
c. Undefined
d. Undefined

80. _____ is a way of expressing a number as a fraction of 100 per cent meaning "per hundred".
a. Percent0
b. Thing
c. Undefined
d. Undefined

81. _____ is an adjective usually refering to being in the centre.
a. Thing
b. Central0
c. Undefined
d. Undefined

Chapter 4. Exponential and Logarithmic Functions

82. A _____ models the S-curve of growth of some set P. The initial stage of growth is approximately exponential; then, as saturation begins, the growth slows, and at maturity, growth stops.
   a. Logistic function0
   b. Thing
   c. Undefined
   d. Undefined

83. A _____ is a numeral used to indicate a count. The most common use of the word today is to name the part of a fraction that tells the number or count of equal parts.
   a. Thing
   b. Numerator0
   c. Undefined
   d. Undefined

84. In mathematics, the concept of a _____ tries to capture the intuitive idea of a geometrical one-dimensional and continuous object. A simple example is the circle.
   a. Thing
   b. Curve0
   c. Undefined
   d. Undefined

85. In elementary algebra, an _____ is a set that contains every real number between two indicated numbers and may contain the two numbers themselves.
   a. Thing
   b. Interval0
   c. Undefined
   d. Undefined

86. A _____ is an individual or household that purchases and uses goods and services generated within the economy.
   a. Thing
   b. Consumer0
   c. Undefined
   d. Undefined

Chapter 4. Exponential and Logarithmic Functions

87. _____ is a statistical time-series measure of a weighted average of prices of a specified set of goods and services purchased by consumers
   a. Consumer price index0
   b. Thing
   c. Undefined
   d. Undefined

88. The word _____ is used in a variety of ways in mathematics.
   a. Thing
   b. Index0
   c. Undefined
   d. Undefined

89. _____ Any process by which a specified characteristic usually amplitude of the output of a device is prevented from exceeding a predetermined value.
   a. Limiting0
   b. Thing
   c. Undefined
   d. Undefined

90. _____ is the chance that something is likely to happen or be the case.
   a. Thing
   b. Probability0
   c. Undefined
   d. Undefined

91. Acid _____ ratio measures the ability of a company to use its near cash or quick assets to immediately extinguish its current liabilities.
   a. Test0
   b. Thing
   c. Undefined
   d. Undefined

92. _____ is the estimation of a physical quantity such as distance, energy, temperature, or time.

Chapter 4. Exponential and Logarithmic Functions

a. Thing
b. Measurement0
c. Undefined
d. Undefined

93. _____ is a decrease that follows an exponential function.
a. Exponential decay0
b. Thing
c. Undefined
d. Undefined

94. In mathematics, an inequality is a statement about the relative size or order of two objects. For example 14 > 10, or 14 is _____ 10.
a. Greater than0
b. Thing
c. Undefined
d. Undefined

95. _____ of a population is the number of childbirths per 1,000 persons per year
a. Birth rate0
b. Thing
c. Undefined
d. Undefined

96. An _____ or member of a set is an object that when collected together make up the set.
a. Element0
b. Thing
c. Undefined
d. Undefined

97. In mathematics, the _____ , or members of a set or more generally a class are all those objects which when collected together make up the set or class.

Chapter 4. Exponential and Logarithmic Functions

    a. Elements0
    b. Thing
    c. Undefined
    d. Undefined

98. _____ is the process in which an unstable atomic nucleus loses energy by emitting radiation in the form of particles or electromagnetic waves.
    a. Radioactive decay0
    b. Thing
    c. Undefined
    d. Undefined

99. A _____ is a type of particle detector that measures ionizing radiation.
    a. Geiger counter0
    b. Thing
    c. Undefined
    d. Undefined

100. _____ of a single or multiple future payments is the nominal amounts of money to change hands at some future date, discounted to account for the time value of money, and other factors such as investment risk.
    a. Present value0
    b. Thing
    c. Undefined
    d. Undefined

101. _____ is a physical property of a system that underlies the common notions of hot and cold; something that is hotter has the greater _____.
    a. Temperature0
    b. Thing
    c. Undefined
    d. Undefined

102. A _____ is an abstract model that uses mathematical language to describe the behavior of a system. Eykhoff defined a _____ as 'a representation of the essential aspects of an existing system which presents knowledge of that system in usable form'.

a. Thing
b. Mathematical model0
c. Undefined
d. Undefined

103. _____ are a measure of time.
a. Thing
b. Minutes0
c. Undefined
d. Undefined

104. Sir Isaac _____, was an English physicist, mathematician, astronomer, natural philosopher, and alchemist, regarded by many as the greatest figure in the history of science
a. Person
b. Newton0
c. Undefined
d. Undefined

105. _____ the expected value of a random variable displays the average or central value of the variable. It is a summary value of the distribution of the variable.
a. Determining0
b. Thing
c. Undefined
d. Undefined

106. In economics, _____ describe market relations between prospective sellers and buyers of a good.
a. Thing
b. Supply and demand0
c. Undefined
d. Undefined

107. In economics, economic _____ is simply a state of the world where economic forces are balanced and in the absence of external influences the values of economic variables will not change.

Chapter 4. Exponential and Logarithmic Functions

   a. Thing
   b. Equilibrium0
   c. Undefined
   d. Undefined

108. A frame of _____ is a particular perspective from which the universe is observed.
   a. Thing
   b. Reference0
   c. Undefined
   d. Undefined

109. In topology and related areas of mathematics a _____ or Moore-Smith sequence is a generalization of a sequence, intended to unify the various notions of limit and generalize them to arbitrary topological spaces.
   a. Thing
   b. Net0
   c. Undefined
   d. Undefined

110. In common philosophical language, a proposition or _____, is the content of an assertion, that is, it is true-or-false and defined by the meaning of a particular piece of language.
   a. Statement0
   b. Concept
   c. Undefined
   d. Undefined

111. _____ is electromagnetic radiation with a wavelength that is visible to the eye (visible _____) or, in a technical or scientific context, electromagnetic radiation of any wavelength.
   a. Light0
   b. Thing
   c. Undefined
   d. Undefined

112. In mathematics, a _____ is a constant multiplicative factor of a certain object. The object can be such things as a variable, a vector, a function, etc. For example, the _____ of $9x^2$ is 9.

Chapter 4. Exponential and Logarithmic Functions 109

   a. Coefficient0
   b. Thing
   c. Undefined
   d. Undefined

113. The metre (or _____, see spelling differences) is a measure of length. It is the basic unit of length in the metric system and in the International System of Units (SI), used around the world for general and scientific purposes.
   a. Meter0
   b. Concept
   c. Undefined
   d. Undefined

114. In geometry, an _____ of a triangle is a straight line through a vertex and perpendicular to (i.e. forming a right angle with) the opposite side or an extension of the opposite side.
   a. Altitude0
   b. Concept
   c. Undefined
   d. Undefined

115. In plane geometry, a _____ is a polygon with four equal sides, four right angles, and parallel opposite sides. In algebra, the _____ of a number is that number multiplied by itself.
   a. Square0
   b. Thing
   c. Undefined
   d. Undefined

116. A _____ is a negotiable instrument instructing a financial institution to pay a specific amount of a specific currency from a specific demand account held in the maker/depositor's name with that institution. Both the maker and payee may be natural persons or legal entities.
   a. Thing
   b. Check0
   c. Undefined
   d. Undefined

117. In the most general sense, a _____ is anything that is a hindrance, or puts individuals at a disadvantage.

a. Liability0
b. Thing
c. Undefined
d. Undefined

118. The _____ of a mathematical object is its size: a property by which it can be larger or smaller than other objects of the same kind; in technical terms, an ordering of the class of objects to which it belongs.
a. Magnitude0
b. Thing
c. Undefined
d. Undefined

119. An _____ is the result from the sudden release of stored energy in the Earth's crust that creates seismic waves.
a. Earthquake0
b. Thing
c. Undefined
d. Undefined

120. In Euclidean geometry, a uniform _____ is a linear transformation that enlargers or diminishes objects, and whose _____ factor is the same in all directions. This is also called homothethy.
a. Thing
b. Scale0
c. Undefined
d. Undefined

121. A _____ is the sum of the elements of a sequence.
a. Series0
b. Thing
c. Undefined
d. Undefined

122. The _____ relative to a specified or implied reference level.

Chapter 4. Exponential and Logarithmic Functions

a. Thing
b. Decibel0
c. Undefined
d. Undefined

123. A _____ is a quantity that denotes the proportional amount or magnitude of one quantity relative to another.
a. Ratio0
b. Thing
c. Undefined
d. Undefined

124. _____ can be defined as the graph depicting the relationship between the price of a certain commodity, and the amount of it that consumers are willing and able to purchase at that given price demand.
a. Demand curve0
b. Thing
c. Undefined
d. Undefined

125. A _____ consists of one quarter of the coordinate plane.
a. Thing
b. Quadrant0
c. Undefined
d. Undefined

126. Transport or _____ is the movement of people and goods from one place to another.
a. Transportation0
b. Thing
c. Undefined
d. Undefined

127. _____ is the design, analysis, and/or construction of works for practical purposes.

Chapter 4. Exponential and Logarithmic Functions

a. Engineering0
b. Thing
c. Undefined
d. Undefined

128. _____ is the calculated approximation of a result which is usable even if input data may be incomplete, uncertain, or noisy.
   a. Concept
   b. Estimation0
   c. Undefined
   d. Undefined

129. _____, in law and economics, is a form of risk management primarily used to hedge against the risk of a contingent loss.
   a. Thing
   b. Insurance0
   c. Undefined
   d. Undefined

130. _____ is a radiometric dating method that uses the naturally occurring isotope carbon-14 to determine the age of carbonaceous materials up to about 60,000 years.
   a. Thing
   b. Radiocarbon dating0
   c. Undefined
   d. Undefined

131. In mathematics, a _____ number (or a _____) is a natural number that has exactly two (distinct) natural number divisors, which are 1 and the _____ number itself.
   a. Thing
   b. Prime0
   c. Undefined
   d. Undefined

132. U.S. liquid _____ is legally defined as 231 cubic inches, and is equal to 3.785411784 litres or abotu 0.13368 cubic feet. This is the most common definition of a _____. The U.S. fluid ounce is defined as 1/128 of a U.S. _____.

a. Gallon0
b. Thing
c. Undefined
d. Undefined

133. A _____, scatter diagram or scatter graph is a graph used in statistics to visually display and relate two quantitative variables of a multidimensional data set by displaying the data as a collection of points, each having one coordinate on a horizontal and one on a vertical axis.
a. Scatterplot0
b. Thing
c. Undefined
d. Undefined

Chapter 5. Integration

1. _____ is a business term for the amount of money that a company receives from its activities in a given period, mostly from sales of products and/or services to customers
   a. Thing
   b. Revenue0
   c. Undefined
   d. Undefined

2. In sociology and biology a _____ is the collection of people or organisms of a particular species living in a given geographic area or space, usually measured by a census.
   a. Thing
   b. Population0
   c. Undefined
   d. Undefined

3. The _____ is a measurement of how a function changes when the values of its inputs change.
   a. Thing
   b. Derivative0
   c. Undefined
   d. Undefined

4. The mathematical concept of a _____ expresses the intuitive idea of deterministic dependence between two quantities, one of which is viewed as primary and the other as secondary. A _____ then is a way to associate a unique output for each input of a specified type, for example, a real number or an element of a given set.
   a. Thing
   b. Function0
   c. Undefined
   d. Undefined

5. _____ in calculus is primitive or indefinite integral of a function f is a function F whose derivative is equal to f, i.e., F Œ = f. The process of solving for antiderivatives is _____
   a. Thing
   b. Antidifferentiation0
   c. Undefined
   d. Undefined

6. _____, a field in mathematics, is the study of how functions change when their inputs change. The primary object of study in _____ is the derivative.

Chapter 5. Integration

   a. Thing
   b. Differential calculus0
   c. Undefined
   d. Undefined

7. In mathematics and the mathematical sciences, a _____ is a fixed, but possibly unspecified, value. This is in contrast to a variable, which is not fixed.
   a. Constant0
   b. Thing
   c. Undefined
   d. Undefined

8. In elementary algebra, an _____ is a set that contains every real number between two indicated numbers and may contain the two numbers themselves.
   a. Thing
   b. Interval0
   c. Undefined
   d. Undefined

9. An _____ of a function f is a function F whose derivative is equal to f, i.e., F' = f.
   a. Antiderivative0
   b. Thing
   c. Undefined
   d. Undefined

10. A _____ is a negotiable instrument instructing a financial institution to pay a specific amount of a specific currency from a specific demand account held in the maker/depositor's name with that institution. Both the maker and payee may be natural persons or legal entities.
   a. Thing
   b. Check0
   c. Undefined
   d. Undefined

11. The _____ of a function is an extension of the concept of a sum, and are identified or found through the use of integration.

a. Integral0
b. Thing
c. Undefined
d. Undefined

12. _____ is a process of combining or accumulating. It may also refer to:
a. Thing
b. Integration0
c. Undefined
d. Undefined

13. In calculus, the indefinite integral of a given function i.e. the set of all antiderivatives of the function is always written with a constant, the _____.
a. Constant of integration0
b. Thing
c. Undefined
d. Undefined

14. One of the three formats applicable to a quadratic function is the _____ which is defined as $f = ax^2 + bx + c$.
a. General form0
b. Thing
c. Undefined
d. Undefined

15. _____ was a German mathematician and philosopher. He invented calculus independently of Newton, and his notation is the one in general use since.
a. Leibniz0
b. Person
c. Undefined
d. Undefined

16. _____ is a function that extends the concept of an ordinary sum

a. Integrand0
   b. Thing
   c. Undefined
   d. Undefined

17. _____ are the basic objects of study in graph theory. Informally speaking, a graph is a set of objects called points, nodes, or vertices connected by links called lines or edges.
   a. Graphs0
   b. Thing
   c. Undefined
   d. Undefined

18. An _____ is when two lines intersect somewhere on a plane creating a right angle at intersection
   a. Axes0
   b. Thing
   c. Undefined
   d. Undefined

19. _____ is often used to describe the measurement of the steepness, incline, gradient, or grade of a straight line. The _____ is defined as the ratio of the "rise" divided by the "run" between two points on a line, or in other words, the ratio of the altitude change to the horizontal distance between any two points on the line.
   a. Slope0
   b. Thing
   c. Undefined
   d. Undefined

20. In trigonometry, the _____ is a function defined as $\tan x = \sin x / \cos x$. The function is so-named because it can be defined as the length of a certain segment of a _____ (in the geometric sense) to the unit circle. In plane geometry, a line is _____ to a curve, at some point, if both line and curve pass through the point with the same direction.
   a. Tangent0
   b. Thing
   c. Undefined
   d. Undefined

21. _____ has two distinct but etymologically-related meanings: one in geometry and one in trigonometry.

a. Thing
b. Tangent line0
c. Undefined
d. Undefined

22. Initial objects are also called _____, and terminal objects are also called final.
a. Thing
b. Coterminal0
c. Undefined
d. Undefined

23. _____ is the change in total cost that arises when the quantity produced changes by one unit.
a. Thing
b. Marginal cost0
c. Undefined
d. Undefined

24. _____ the expected value of a random variable displays the average or central value of the variable. It is a summary value of the distribution of the variable.
a. Thing
b. Determining0
c. Undefined
d. Undefined

25. In mathematics, a _____ is the result of multiplying, or an expression that identifies factors to be multiplied.
a. Product0
b. Thing
c. Undefined
d. Undefined

26. _____ is the extra revenue that an additional unit of product will bring a firm. It can also be described as the change in total revenue/change in number of units sold.

Chapter 5. Integration

a. Marginal revenue0
b. Thing
c. Undefined
d. Undefined

27. Fixed costs are expenses whose total does not change in proportion to the activity of a business.Unit fixed costs decline with volume following a retangular hyperbola as the volume of production.Variable costs by contrast change in relation to the activity of a business such as sales or production volume.Along with variable costs,fixed costs make up one of the two components of total cost. In the most simple production function total cost is equal to fixed costs plus variable costs.In accounting terminology, fixed costs will broadly include all costs which are not included in cost of goods sold, and variable costs are those captured in costs of goods sold. The implicit assumption required to make the equivalence between the accounting and economics terminology is that the accounting period is equal to the period in which fixed costs do not vary in relation to production. In practice, this equivalence does not always hold and depending on the period under consideration by management, some overhead expenses can be adjusted by management, and the specific allocation of each expense to each category will be decided under cost accounting.In business planning and management accounting, usage of the terms fixed costs, variable costs and others will often differ from usage in economics, and may depend on the intended use. For example, costs may be segregated into per unit costs fixed costs per period, and variable costs as a proportion of revenue. Capital expenditures will usually be allocated separately, and depending on the purpose, a portion may be regularly allocated to expenses as depreciation and amortization and seen as a _____ per period, or the entire amount may be considered upfront fixed costs.
   a. Thing
   b. Fixed cost0
   c. Undefined
   d. Undefined

28. _____ are expenses whose total does not change in proportion to the activity of a business, within the relevant time period or scale of production
   a. Fixed costs0
   b. Thing
   c. Undefined
   d. Undefined

29. The _____ of measurement are a globally standardized and modernized form of the metric system.
   a. Thing
   b. Units0
   c. Undefined
   d. Undefined

30. A _____ is an individual or household that purchases and uses goods and services generated within the economy.
   a. Consumer0
   b. Thing
   c. Undefined
   d. Undefined

31. A _____ is a special kind of ratio, indicating a relationship between two measurements with different units, such as miles to gallons or cents to pounds.
   a. Rate0
   b. Thing
   c. Undefined
   d. Undefined

32. In economics, supply and _____ describe market relations between prospective sellers and buyers of a good.
   a. Demand0
   b. Thing
   c. Undefined
   d. Undefined

33. _____ is defined as the rate of change or derivative with respect to time of velocity.
   a. Thing
   b. Acceleration0
   c. Undefined
   d. Undefined

34. _____ is the level of functional and/or metabolic efficiency of an organism at both the micro level.
   a. Thing
   b. Health0
   c. Undefined
   d. Undefined

35. In the scientific method, an _____ (Latin: ex-+-periri, "of (or from) trying"), is a set of actions and observations, performed in the context of solving a particular problem or question, in order to support or falsify a hypothesis or research concerning phenomena.

a. Experiment0
b. Thing
c. Undefined
d. Undefined

36. _____ are a measure of time.
   a. Minutes0
   b. Thing
   c. Undefined
   d. Undefined

37. In mathematics, the concept of a _____ tries to capture the intuitive idea of a geometrical one-dimensional and continuous object. A simple example is the circle.
   a. Curve0
   b. Thing
   c. Undefined
   d. Undefined

38. _____ is an extension of the concept of a sum.
   a. Thing
   b. Definite integral0
   c. Undefined
   d. Undefined

39. In geometry, a _____ is defined as a quadrilateral where all four of its angles are right angles.
   a. Rectangle0
   b. Thing
   c. Undefined
   d. Undefined

40. A _____ is a quadrilateral, which is defined as a shape with four sides, which has a pair of parallel sides.

a. Thing
b. Trapezoid0
c. Undefined
d. Undefined

41. A _____ is one of the basic shapes of geometry: a polygon with three vertices and three sides which are straight line segments.
   a. Thing
   b. Triangle0
   c. Undefined
   d. Undefined

42. A _____ is the result of the addition of a set of numbers. The numbers may be natural numbers, complex numbers, matrices, or still more complicated objects. An infinite _____ is a subtle procedure known as a series.
   a. Sum0
   b. Thing
   c. Undefined
   d. Undefined

43. In mathematics, a _____ is a mathematical statement which appears likely to be true, but has not been formally proven to be true under the rules of mathematical logic.
   a. Conjecture0
   b. Concept
   c. Undefined
   d. Undefined

44. A _____ function is a function for which, intuitively, small changes in the input result in small changes in the output.
   a. Continuous0
   b. Event
   c. Undefined
   d. Undefined

45. The _____ integers are all the integers from zero on upwards.

Chapter 5. Integration　　123

   a. Thing
   b. Nonnegative0
   c. Undefined
   d. Undefined

46. In mathematics, a _____ is a statement that can be proved on the basis of explicitly stated or previously agreed assumptions.
   a. Theorem0
   b. Thing
   c. Undefined
   d. Undefined

47. In a mathematical proof or a syllogism, a _____ is a statement that is the logical consequence of preceding statements.
   a. Concept
   b. Conclusion0
   c. Undefined
   d. Undefined

48. _____ is the mathematical action of repeatedly adding or subtracting one, usually to find out how many objects there are or to set aside a desired number of objects.
   a. Counting0
   b. Thing
   c. Undefined
   d. Undefined

49. In plane geometry, a _____ is a polygon with four equal sides, four right angles, and parallel opposite sides. In algebra, the _____ of a number is that number multiplied by itself.
   a. Thing
   b. Square0
   c. Undefined
   d. Undefined

50. Mathematical _____ is used to represent ideas.

a. Thing
b. Notation0
c. Undefined
d. Undefined

51. The plus and _____ signs are mathematical symbols used to represent the notions of positive and negative as well as the operations of addition and subtraction.
a. Thing
b. Minus0
c. Undefined
d. Undefined

52. In geographic information systems, a _____ comprises an entity with a geographic location, typically determined by points, arcs, or polygons. Carriageways and cadastres exemplify _____ data.
a. Thing
b. Feature0
c. Undefined
d. Undefined

53. _____, in economics and political economy, are the distributions or payments awarded to the various suppliers of the factors of production.
a. Thing
b. Returns0
c. Undefined
d. Undefined

54. An _____ is a combination of numbers, operators, grouping symbols and/or free variables and bound variables arranged in a meaningful way which can be evaluated..
a. Expression0
b. Thing
c. Undefined
d. Undefined

55. _____ is the addition of a set of numbers; the result is their sum. The "numbers" to be summed may be natural numbers, complex numbers, matrices, or still more complicated objects. An infinite sum is a subtle procedure known as a series.

Chapter 5. Integration

a. Thing
b. Summation0
c. Undefined
d. Undefined

56. _____ is a mathematical subject that includes the study of limits, derivatives, integrals, and power series and constitutes a major part of modern university curriculum.
   a. Calculus0
   b. Thing
   c. Undefined
   d. Undefined

57. In number theory, the _____ of arithmetic (or unique factorization theorem) states that every natural number greater than 1 can be written as a unique product of prime numbers.
   a. Concept
   b. Fundamental theorem0
   c. Undefined
   d. Undefined

58. In mathematics, the _____ of a function is the set of all "output" values produced by that function. Given a function $f : A \to B$, the _____ of f, is defined to be the set $\{x \in B : x = f(a) \text{ for some } a \in A\}$.
   a. Range0
   b. Thing
   c. Undefined
   d. Undefined

59. _____ is a physical property of a system that underlies the common notions of hot and cold; something that is hotter has the greater _____.
   a. Temperature0
   b. Thing
   c. Undefined
   d. Undefined

60. In mathematics, a _____ of a k-place relation $L \subseteq X_1 \times \ldots \times X_k$ is one of the sets X_j, $1 \leq j \leq k$. In the special case where k = 2 and $L \subseteq X_1 \times X_2$ is a function $L : X_1 \to X_2$, it is conventional to refer to X_1 as the _____ of the function and to refer to X_2 as the codomain of the function.

126 *Chapter 5. Integration*

   a. Domain0
   b. Thing
   c. Undefined
   d. Undefined

61. In mathematics, an _____, mean, or central tendency of a data set refers to a measure of the "middle" or "expected" value of the data set.
   a. Average0
   b. Concept
   c. Undefined
   d. Undefined

62. In astronomy, geography, geometry and related sciences and contexts, a plane is said to be _____ at a given point if it is locally perpendicular to the gradient of the gravity field, i.e., with the direction of the gravitational force at that point.
   a. Thing
   b. Horizontal0
   c. Undefined
   d. Undefined

63. The _____ of a solid object is the three-dimensional concept of how much space it occupies, often quantified numerically.
   a. Thing
   b. Volume0
   c. Undefined
   d. Undefined

64. The _____, the average in everyday English, which is also called the arithmetic _____ (and is distinguished from the geometric _____ or harmonic _____). The average is also called the sample _____. The expected value of a random variable, which is also called the population _____.
   a. Thing
   b. Mean0
   c. Undefined
   d. Undefined

Chapter 5. Integration

65. _____, from Latin meaning "to make progress", is defined in two different ways. Pure economic _____ is the increase in wealth that an investor has from making an investment, taking into consideration all costs associated with that investment including the opportunity cost of capital.
   a. Thing
   b. Profit0
   c. Undefined
   d. Undefined

66. _____ of an object is its speed in a particular direction.
   a. Velocity0
   b. Thing
   c. Undefined
   d. Undefined

67. In mathematics, there are several meanings of _____ depending on the subject.
   a. Degree0
   b. Thing
   c. Undefined
   d. Undefined

68. In business, particularly accounting, a _____ is the time intervals that the accounts, statement, payments, or other calculations cover.
   a. Thing
   b. Period0
   c. Undefined
   d. Undefined

69. The _____ refers to a relationship between the duration of learning or experience and the resulting progress
   a. Thing
   b. Learning curve0
   c. Undefined
   d. Undefined

70. Acid _____ ratio measures the ability of a company to use its near cash or quick assets to immediately extinguish its current liabilities.

a. Thing
b. Test0
c. Undefined
d. Undefined

71. _____ the American term is a way to approximately calculate the definite integral
a. Trapezoidal Rule0
b. Thing
c. Undefined
d. Undefined

72. A _____ defined function f(x) of a real variable x is a function whose definition is given differently on disjoint subsets of its domain.
a. Piecewise0
b. Thing
c. Undefined
d. Undefined

73. In mathematics, the _____ of two sets A and B is the set that contains all elements of A that also belong to B (or equivalently, all elements of B that also belong to A), but no other elements.
a. Thing
b. Intersection0
c. Undefined
d. Undefined

74. In mathematics, _____ are the intuitive idea of a geometrical one-dimensional and continuous object.
a. Curves0
b. Thing
c. Undefined
d. Undefined

75. In mathematical analysis and related areas of mathematics, a set is called _____, if it is, in a certain sense, of finite size.

Chapter 5. Integration

a. Thing
b. Bounded0
c. Undefined
d. Undefined

76. A _____ is a set of numbers that designate location in a given reference system, such as x,y in a planar _____ system or an x,y,z in a three-dimensional _____ system.
   a. Thing
   b. Coordinate0
   c. Undefined
   d. Undefined

77. The _____ is the highest point in a certain portion of a graph.
   a. Thing
   b. Relative maximum0
   c. Undefined
   d. Undefined

78. In geometry, the _____ of an object is a point in some sense in the middle of the object.
   a. Center0
   b. Thing
   c. Undefined
   d. Undefined

79. In classical geometry, a _____ of a circle or sphere is any line segment from its center to its boundary. By extension, the _____ of a circle or sphere is the length of any such segment. The _____ is half the diameter. In science and engineering the term _____ of curvature is commonly used as a synonym for _____.
   a. Radius0
   b. Thing
   c. Undefined
   d. Undefined

80. _____ is the flow of blood in the cardiovascular system.

a. Blood flow0
b. Thing
c. Undefined
d. Undefined

81. _____ is a tool for finding antiderivatives and integrals. Using the fundamental theorem of calculus often requires finding an antiderivative. For this and other reasons, this rule is a relatively important tool for mathematicians. It is the counterpart to the chain rule of differentiation.
a. Thing
b. Integration by substitution0
c. Undefined
d. Undefined

82. In calculus, the _____ is a formula for the derivative of the composite of two functions.
a. Concept
b. Chain rule0
c. Undefined
d. Undefined

83. A _____ is a symbolic representation denoting a quantity or expression. It often represents an "unknown" quantity that has the potential to change.
a. Thing
b. Variable0
c. Undefined
d. Undefined

84. The _____ governs the differentiation of products of differentiable functions.
a. Product rule0
b. Thing
c. Undefined
d. Undefined

85. In mathematics, factorization (British English: factorisation) or factoring is the decomposition of an object (for example, a number, a polynomial, or a matrix) into a product of other objects, or _____, which when multiplied together give the original.

a. Thing
b. Factors0
c. Undefined
d. Undefined

86. _____ is a kind of property which exists as magnitude or multitude. It is among the basic classes of things along with quality, substance, change, and relation.
a. Thing
b. Amount0
c. Undefined
d. Undefined

87. _____ is the chance that something is likely to happen or be the case.
a. Thing
b. Probability0
c. Undefined
d. Undefined

88. A frame of _____ is a particular perspective from which the universe is observed.
a. Thing
b. Reference0
c. Undefined
d. Undefined

89. _____ is a synonym for information.
a. Thing
b. Data0
c. Undefined
d. Undefined

90. _____ are the day-to-day expenses incurred in running a business, such as sales and administration, or research & development, as opposed to Production, costs, and pricing.

a. Operating expenses0
b. Thing
c. Undefined
d. Undefined

91. A _____ is a statement or claimt that a particular event will occur in the future in more certain terms than a forecast.
a. Thing
b. Prediction0
c. Undefined
d. Undefined

92. _____ (Groups, Algorithms and Programming) is a computer algebra system for computational discrete algebra with particular emphasis on, but not restricted to, computational group theory.
a. Thing
b. Gap0
c. Undefined
d. Undefined

93. A _____, scatter diagram or scatter graph is a graph used in statistics to visually display and relate two quantitative variables of a multidimensional data set by displaying the data as a collection of points, each having one coordinate on a horizontal and one on a vertical axis.
a. Scatterplot0
b. Thing
c. Undefined
d. Undefined

94. In mathematics and elsewhere, the adjective _____ means fourth order, such as the function x4. A _____ number is a number which equals the fourth power of an integer.
a. Quartic0
b. Thing
c. Undefined
d. Undefined

95. The word _____ comes from the Latin word linearis, which means created by lines.

a. Thing
b. Linear0
c. Undefined
d. Undefined

96. In mathematics, a _____ is an expression that is constructed from one or more variables and constants, using only the operations of addition, subtraction, multiplication, and constant positive whole number exponents. is a _____. Note in particular that division by an expression containing a variable is not in general allowed in polynomials. [1]
    a. Polynomial0
    b. Thing
    c. Undefined
    d. Undefined

1. _____ is the chance that something is likely to happen or be the case.
   a. Thing
   b. Probability0
   c. Undefined
   d. Undefined

2. _____ is a measure of difference for interval and ratio variables between the observed value and the mean.
   a. Thing
   b. Deviation0
   c. Undefined
   d. Undefined

3. The _____ of measurement are a globally standardized and modernized form of the metric system.
   a. Units0
   b. Thing
   c. Undefined
   d. Undefined

4. A _____ is an individual or household that purchases and uses goods and services generated within the economy.
   a. Thing
   b. Consumer0
   c. Undefined
   d. Undefined

5. In mathematics, the concept of a _____ tries to capture the intuitive idea of a geometrical one-dimensional and continuous object. A simple example is the circle.
   a. Thing
   b. Curve0
   c. Undefined
   d. Undefined

6. In economics, supply and _____ describe market relations between prospective sellers and buyers of a good.

a. Thing
b. Demand0
c. Undefined
d. Undefined

7. _____ can be defined as the graph depicting the relationship between the price of a certain commodity, and the amount of it that consumers are willing and able to purchase at that given price demand.
a. Thing
b. Demand curve0
c. Undefined
d. Undefined

8. In mathematics, _____ are the intuitive idea of a geometrical one-dimensional and continuous object.
a. Thing
b. Curves0
c. Undefined
d. Undefined

9. In economics, economic _____ is simply a state of the world where economic forces are balanced and in the absence of external influences the values of economic variables will not change.
a. Thing
b. Equilibrium0
c. Undefined
d. Undefined

10. In mathematics, the _____ of two sets A and B is the set that contains all elements of A that also belong to B (or equivalently, all elements of B that also belong to A), but no other elements.
a. Intersection0
b. Thing
c. Undefined
d. Undefined

11. The mathematical concept of a _____ expresses the intuitive idea of deterministic dependence between two quantities, one of which is viewed as primary and the other as secondary. A _____ then is a way to associate a unique output for each input of a specified type, for example, a real number or an element of a given set.

a. Function0
b. Thing
c. Undefined
d. Undefined

12. In mathematics, a _____ is the result of multiplying, or an expression that identifies factors to be multiplied.
a. Product0
b. Thing
c. Undefined
d. Undefined

13. _____ is a kind of property which exists as magnitude or multitude. It is among the basic classes of things along with quality, substance, change, and relation.
a. Thing
b. Amount0
c. Undefined
d. Undefined

14. In mathematics, an _____, mean, or central tendency of a data set refers to a measure of the "middle" or "expected" value of the data set.
a. Average0
b. Concept
c. Undefined
d. Undefined

15. A _____ is a function that assigns a number to subsets of a given set.
a. Thing
b. Measure0
c. Undefined
d. Undefined

16. _____ is a business term for the amount of money that a company receives from its activities in a given period, mostly from sales of products and/or services to customers

a. Revenue0
b. Thing
c. Undefined
d. Undefined

17. In finance and economics, _____ is the process of finding the present value of an amount of cash at some future date, and along with compounding cash forms the basis of time value of money calculations.
   a. Discount0
   b. Thing
   c. Undefined
   d. Undefined

18. A _____ is one of the basic shapes of geometry: a polygon with three vertices and three sides which are straight line segments.
   a. Thing
   b. Triangle0
   c. Undefined
   d. Undefined

19. _____, from Latin meaning "to make progress", is defined in two different ways. Pure economic _____ is the increase in wealth that an investor has from making an investment, taking into consideration all costs associated with that investment including the opportunity cost of capital.
   a. Thing
   b. Profit0
   c. Undefined
   d. Undefined

20. The plus and _____ signs are mathematical symbols used to represent the notions of positive and negative as well as the operations of addition and subtraction.
   a. Thing
   b. Minus0
   c. Undefined
   d. Undefined

21. In economics, _____ describe market relations between prospective sellers and buyers of a good.

Chapter 6. Applications of Integration

   a. Supply and demand0
   b. Thing
   c. Undefined
   d. Undefined

22. _____ is a synonym for information.
   a. Thing
   b. Data0
   c. Undefined
   d. Undefined

23. A _____, scatter diagram or scatter graph is a graph used in statistics to visually display and relate two quantitative variables of a multidimensional data set by displaying the data as a collection of points, each having one coordinate on a horizontal and one on a vertical axis.
   a. Thing
   b. Scatterplot0
   c. Undefined
   d. Undefined

24. _____ in technical analysis is typical price multiplied by volume, a kind of approximation to the dollar value of a day's trading.
   a. Thing
   b. Money flow0
   c. Undefined
   d. Undefined

25. A _____ function is a function for which, intuitively, small changes in the input result in small changes in the output.
   a. Event
   b. Continuous0
   c. Undefined
   d. Undefined

26. _____ is the fee paid on borrowed money.

Chapter 6. Applications of Integration

a. Thing
b. Interest0
c. Undefined
d. Undefined

27. Initial objects are also called _____, and terminal objects are also called final.
a. Coterminal0
b. Thing
c. Undefined
d. Undefined

28. A _____ is a special kind of ratio, indicating a relationship between two measurements with different units, such as miles to gallons or cents to pounds.
a. Thing
b. Rate0
c. Undefined
d. Undefined

29. A _____ are accounts maintained by commercial banks, savings and loan associations, credit unions, and mutual savings banks that pay interest but can not be used directly as money by, for example, writing a cheque.
a. Thing
b. Savings account0
c. Undefined
d. Undefined

30. In banking and accountancy, the outstanding _____ is the amount of money owned, or due, that remains in a deposit account or a loan account at a given date, after all past remittances, payments and withdrawal have been accounted for.
a. Thing
b. Balance0
c. Undefined
d. Undefined

31. An _____ is the fee paid on borrow money.

Chapter 6. Applications of Integration

a. Interest rate0
b. Concept
c. Undefined
d. Undefined

32. _____ or investing is a term with several closely-related meanings in business management, finance and economics, related to saving or deferring consumption.
a. Thing
b. Investment0
c. Undefined
d. Undefined

33. The _____ of a function is an extension of the concept of a sum, and are identified or found through the use of integration.
a. Integral0
b. Thing
c. Undefined
d. Undefined

34. In elementary algebra, an _____ is a set that contains every real number between two indicated numbers and may contain the two numbers themselves.
a. Interval0
b. Thing
c. Undefined
d. Undefined

35. In mathematics a _____ is a function which defines a distance between elements of a set.
a. Metric0
b. Thing
c. Undefined
d. Undefined

36. _____ is the logarithm to the base e, where e is an irrational constant approximately equal to 2.718281828459.

Chapter 6. Applications of Integration

a. Natural logarithm0
b. Thing
c. Undefined
d. Undefined

37. In mathematics, a _____ of a number x is the exponent y of the power by such that $x = b^y$. The value used for the base b must be neither 0 nor 1, nor a root of 1 in the case of the extension to complex numbers, and is typically 10, e, or 2.

a. Logarithm0
b. Thing
c. Undefined
d. Undefined

38. _____ is a way of expressing a number as a fraction of 100 per cent meaning "per hundred".

a. Percent0
b. Thing
c. Undefined
d. Undefined

39. _____ of a single or multiple future payments is the nominal amounts of money to change hands at some future date, discounted to account for the time value of money, and other factors such as investment risk.

a. Thing
b. Present value0
c. Undefined
d. Undefined

40. A _____ is a symbolic representation denoting a quantity or expression. It often represents an "unknown" quantity that has the potential to change.

a. Thing
b. Variable0
c. Undefined
d. Undefined

41. In mathematics and the mathematical sciences, a _____ is a fixed, but possibly unspecified, value. This is in contrast to a variable, which is not fixed.

a. Thing
b. Constant0
c. Undefined
d. Undefined

42. _____ is a function whose values do not vary and thus are constant.
a. Thing
b. Constant function0
c. Undefined
d. Undefined

43. In business, particularly accounting, a _____ is the time intervals that the accounts, statement, payments, or other calculations cover.
a. Thing
b. Period0
c. Undefined
d. Undefined

44. _____ are economic entities that give rise to future economic benefit and is controlled by the entity as a result of past transaction or other events
a. Thing
b. Asset0
c. Undefined
d. Undefined

45. In mathematics, _____ growth occurs when the growth rate of a function is always proportional to the function's current size.
a. Exponential0
b. Thing
c. Undefined
d. Undefined

46. _____ is essentially exponential growth based on a constant rate of compound interest.

Chapter 6. Applications of Integration

a. Thing
b. Exponential growth model0
c. Undefined
d. Undefined

47. An _____ is the limit of a definite integral, as an endpoint of the interval of integration approaches either a specified real number or ‡ or − ‡ or, in some cases, as both endpoints approach limits.
    a. Improper integral0
    b. Thing
    c. Undefined
    d. Undefined

48. _____ is the state of being greater than any finite real or natural number, however large.
    a. Infinite0
    b. Thing
    c. Undefined
    d. Undefined

49. _____ is the state of being greater than any finite number, however large.
    a. Infinity0
    b. Thing
    c. Undefined
    d. Undefined

50. In mathematics, a set is called _____ if there is a bijection between the set and some set of the form {1, 2, ..., n} where n is a natural number.
    a. Finite0
    b. Thing
    c. Undefined
    d. Undefined

51. In mathematics, _____ describes an entity with a limit.

a. Convergent0
b. Thing
c. Undefined
d. Undefined

52. In mathematics, a _____ series is an infinite series that is not convergent, meaning that the infinite sequence of the partial sums of the series does not have a limit.
   a. Thing
   b. Divergent0
   c. Undefined
   d. Undefined

53. _____ Any process by which a specified characteristic usually amplitude of the output of a device is prevented from exceeding a predetermined value.
   a. Thing
   b. Limiting0
   c. Undefined
   d. Undefined

54. An _____ is when two lines intersect somewhere on a plane creating a right angle at intersection
   a. Thing
   b. Axes0
   c. Undefined
   d. Undefined

55. In mathematical analysis and related areas of mathematics, a set is called _____, if it is, in a certain sense, of finite size.
   a. Thing
   b. Bounded0
   c. Undefined
   d. Undefined

56. In mathematics, the word _____ is used informally to refer to certain distinct bodies of knowledge about mathematics.

Chapter 6. Applications of Integration

a. Theoretical0
b. Thing
c. Undefined
d. Undefined

57. _____ is the branch of mathematics concerned with analysis of random phenomena. The central objects of theoretical probabiltiy are random variables, stochastic processes, and events: mathematical abstractions of non-deterministic events or measured quantities that may either be single occurrences or evolve over time in an apparently random fashion.
    a. Theoretical probability0
    b. Thing
    c. Undefined
    d. Undefined

58. Deductive _____ is the kind of _____ in which the conclusion is necessitated by, or reached from, previously known facts (the premises).
    a. Thing
    b. Reasoning0
    c. Undefined
    d. Undefined

59. _____ is a function that represents a probability distribution in terms of integrals.
    a. Probability density function0
    b. Thing
    c. Undefined
    d. Undefined

60. _____ is mass m per unit volume V.
    a. Density0
    b. Thing
    c. Undefined
    d. Undefined

61. _____ is a mathematical subject that includes the study of limits, derivatives, integrals, and power series and constitutes a major part of modern university curriculum.

a. Thing
b. Calculus0
c. Undefined
d. Undefined

62. The _____ integers are all the integers from zero on upwards.
a. Nonnegative0
b. Thing
c. Undefined
d. Undefined

63. In mathematics, the _____ of a function is the set of all "output" values produced by that function. Given a function $f : A \to B$, the _____ of f, is defined to be the set $\{x \in B : x = f(a) \text{ for some } a \in A\}$.
a. Thing
b. Range0
c. Undefined
d. Undefined

64. The _____ relative to a specified or implied reference level.
a. Decibel0
b. Thing
c. Undefined
d. Undefined

65. _____ is a quantity whose values are random and to which a probability distribution is assigned.
a. Random variable0
b. Thing
c. Undefined
d. Undefined

66. In mathematical analysis, _____ are objects which generalize functions and probability distributions.

Chapter 6. Applications of Integration

a. Distribution0
b. Thing
c. Undefined
d. Undefined

67. Transport or _____ is the movement of people and goods from one place to another.
a. Thing
b. Transportation0
c. Undefined
d. Undefined

68. A _____ is a one-dimensional picture in which the integers are shown as specially-marked points evenly spaced on a line.
a. Thing
b. Number line0
c. Undefined
d. Undefined

69. In the scientific method, an _____ (Latin: ex-+-periri, "of (or from) trying"), is a set of actions and observations, performed in the context of solving a particular problem or question, in order to support or falsify a hypothesis or research concerning phenomena.
a. Experiment0
b. Thing
c. Undefined
d. Undefined

70. In probability theory the _____ .
a. Expected value0
b. Thing
c. Undefined
d. Undefined

71. The _____, the average in everyday English, which is also called the arithmetic _____ (and is distinguished from the geometric _____ or harmonic _____). The average is also called the sample _____. The expected value of a random variable, which is also called the population _____.

Chapter 6. Applications of Integration

   a. Thing
   b. Mean0
   c. Undefined
   d. Undefined

72. _____ of a random variable or somewhat more precisely, of a probability distribution is a measure of its statistical dispersion, indicating how its possible values are spread around the expected value.
   a. Variance0
   b. Thing
   c. Undefined
   d. Undefined

73. _____ of a probability distribution, random variable, or population or multiset of values is a measure of the spread of its values.
   a. Thing
   b. Standard deviation0
   c. Undefined
   d. Undefined

74. In mathematics, a _____ in elementary terms is any of a variety of different functions from geometry, such as rotations, reflections and translations.
   a. Thing
   b. Transformation0
   c. Undefined
   d. Undefined

75. The _____, also called Gaussian distribution by scientists , is a continuous probability distribution of great importance in many fields.
   a. Normal distribution0
   b. Thing
   c. Undefined
   d. Undefined

76. _____, also called Gaussian distribution by scientists, is a continuous probability distribution of great importance in many fields.

Chapter 6. Applications of Integration

a. Normal distributions0
b. Thing
c. Undefined
d. Undefined

77. _____ is the amount of time someone works beyond normal working hours.
a. Compensatory time0
b. Thing
c. Undefined
d. Undefined

78. _____ that assigns a probability to every subset of its state space in such a way that the probability axioms are satisfied.
a. Thing
b. Probability distribution0
c. Undefined
d. Undefined

79. _____ is the application of tools and a processing medium to the transformation of raw materials into finished goods for sale.
a. Manufacturing0
b. Thing
c. Undefined
d. Undefined

80. A central concept in science and the scientific method is that all evidence must be _____, or empirically based, that is, dependent on evidence or consequences that are observable by the senses.
a. Empirical0
b. Thing
c. Undefined
d. Undefined

81. In descriptive statistics, using the _____ is a way of providing estimation of proportions of the data that should fall above and below a given value.

150 Chapter 6. Applications of Integration

a. Percentile0
b. Thing
c. Undefined
d. Undefined

82. Acid _____ ratio measures the ability of a company to use its near cash or quick assets to immediately extinguish its current liabilities.
a. Thing
b. Test0
c. Undefined
d. Undefined

83. In probability theory and statistics, a _____ is a number dividing the higher half of a sample, a population, or a probability distribution from the lower half.
a. Median0
b. Concept
c. Undefined
d. Undefined

84. _____ is a process of combining or accumulating. It may also refer to:
a. Integration0
b. Thing
c. Undefined
d. Undefined

85. An _____ of a function f is a function F whose derivative is equal to f, i.e., F' = f.
a. Antiderivative0
b. Thing
c. Undefined
d. Undefined

86. In mathematics, _____ geometry was the traditional name for the geometry of three-dimensional Euclidean space — for practical purposes the kind of space we live in.

a. Solid0
b. Thing
c. Undefined
d. Undefined

87. In mathematics, a _____ is a two-dimensional manifold or surface that is perfectly flat.
a. Thing
b. Plane0
c. Undefined
d. Undefined

88. The _____ of a solid object is the three-dimensional concept of how much space it occupies, often quantified numerically.
a. Volume0
b. Thing
c. Undefined
d. Undefined

89. A _____ is the result of the addition of a set of numbers. The numbers may be natural numbers, complex numbers, matrices, or still more complicated objects. An infinite _____ is a subtle procedure known as a series.
a. Thing
b. Sum0
c. Undefined
d. Undefined

90. In mathematics, a _____ is a quadric surface, with the following equation in Cartesian coordinates: $(x/a)^2 + (y/b)^2 = 1$.
a. Cylinder0
b. Thing
c. Undefined
d. Undefined

91. In geometry, an _____ is a point at which a line segment or ray terminates.

Chapter 6. Applications of Integration

　a. Thing
　b. Endpoint0
　c. Undefined
　d. Undefined

92. In classical geometry, a _____ of a circle or sphere is any line segment from its center to its boundary. By extension, the _____ of a circle or sphere is the length of any such segment. The _____ is half the diameter. In science and engineering the term _____ of curvature is commonly used as a synonym for _____.
　a. Radius0
　b. Thing
　c. Undefined
　d. Undefined

93. _____ is an extension of the concept of a sum.
　a. Thing
　b. Definite integral0
　c. Undefined
　d. Undefined

94. A _____ is a function for which, intuitively, small changes in the input result in small changes in the output.
　a. Continuous function0
　b. Event
　c. Undefined
　d. Undefined

95. In mathematics, a _____ is a statement that can be proved on the basis of explicitly stated or previously agreed assumptions.
　a. Thing
　b. Theorem0
　c. Undefined
　d. Undefined

96. In mathematics, a _____ is the set of all points in three-dimensional space (R^3) which are at distance r from a fixed point of that space, where r is a positive real number called the radius of the _____. The fixed point is called the center or centre, and is not part of the _____ itself.

a. Thing
b. Sphere0
c. Undefined
d. Undefined

97. A _____ is traditionally an infinitesimally small change in a variable.
a. Thing
b. Differential0
c. Undefined
d. Undefined

98. A _____ is a mathematical equation for an unknown function of one or several variables which relates the values of the function itself and of its derivatives of various orders.
a. Thing
b. Differential equation0
c. Undefined
d. Undefined

99. The _____ is a measurement of how a function changes when the values of its inputs change.
a. Thing
b. Derivative0
c. Undefined
d. Undefined

100. In sociology and biology a _____ is the collection of people or organisms of a particular species living in a given geographic area or space, usually measured by a census.
a. Thing
b. Population0
c. Undefined
d. Undefined

101. In mathematics, a _____ is the end result of a division problem. It can also be expressed as the number of times the divisor divides into the dividend.

Chapter 6. Applications of Integration

a. Thing
b. Quotient0
c. Undefined
d. Undefined

102. An _____ is a combination of numbers, operators, grouping symbols and/or free variables and bound variables arranged in a meaningful way which can be evaluated..
a. Thing
b. Expression0
c. Undefined
d. Undefined

103. In geometry, an _____ of a triangle is a straight line through a vertex and perpendicular to (i.e. forming a right angle with) the opposite side or an extension of the opposite side.
a. Concept
b. Altitude0
c. Undefined
d. Undefined

104. _____ are the basic objects of study in graph theory. Informally speaking, a graph is a set of objects called points, nodes, or vertices connected by links called lines or edges.
a. Thing
b. Graphs0
c. Undefined
d. Undefined

105. A _____ is a quantity that denotes the proportional amount or magnitude of one quantity relative to another.
a. Thing
b. Ratio0
c. Undefined
d. Undefined

106. A _____ is a unit of length, usually used to measure distance, in a number of different systems, including Imperial units, United States customary units and Norwegian/Swedish mil. Its size can vary from system to system, but in each is between 1 and 10 kilometers. In contemporary English contexts _____ refers to either:

Chapter 6. Applications of Integration

a. Thing
b. Mile0
c. Undefined
d. Undefined

107. U.S. liquid _____ is legally defined as 231 cubic inches, and is equal to 3.785411784 litres or abotu 0.13368 cubic feet. This is the most common definition of a _____. The U.S. fluid ounce is defined as 1/128 of a U.S. _____.
a. Thing
b. Gallon0
c. Undefined
d. Undefined

108. _____ is the extra revenue that an additional unit of product will bring a firm. It can also be described as the change in total revenue/change in number of units sold.
a. Thing
b. Marginal revenue0
c. Undefined
d. Undefined

109. _____ is the change in total cost that arises when the quantity produced changes by one unit.
a. Marginal cost0
b. Thing
c. Undefined
d. Undefined

110. A frame of _____ is a particular perspective from which the universe is observed.
a. Reference0
b. Thing
c. Undefined
d. Undefined

111. In geographic information systems, a _____ comprises an entity with a geographic location, typically determined by points, arcs, or polygons. Carriageways and cadastres exemplify _____ data.

a. Thing
b. Feature0
c. Undefined
d. Undefined

112. In mathematics, a _____ is an expression that is constructed from one or more variables and constants, using only the operations of addition, subtraction, multiplication, and constant positive whole number exponents. is a _____. Note in particular that division by an expression containing a variable is not in general allowed in polynomials. [1]
a. Polynomial0
b. Thing
c. Undefined
d. Undefined

113. A _____ is 360° or 2δ radians.
a. Turn0
b. Thing
c. Undefined
d. Undefined

114. _____ is the estimation of a physical quantity such as distance, energy, temperature, or time.
a. Measurement0
b. Thing
c. Undefined
d. Undefined

115. _____ is the ability to hold, receive or absorb, or a measure thereof, similar to the concept of volume.
a. Capacity0
b. Concept
c. Undefined
d. Undefined

Chapter 7. Functions of Several Variables

1. In Euclidean geometry, an _____ is a closed segment of a differentiable curve in the two-dimensional plane; for example, a circular _____ is a segment of a circle.
   a. Arc0
   b. Concept
   c. Undefined
   d. Undefined

2. A _____ of a number is the product of that number with any integer.
   a. Multiple0
   b. Thing
   c. Undefined
   d. Undefined

3. A _____ is a symbolic representation denoting a quantity or expression. It often represents an "unknown" quantity that has the potential to change.
   a. Thing
   b. Variable0
   c. Undefined
   d. Undefined

4. _____ are a method for finding the extrema of a function of several variables subject to one or more constraints: it is the basic tool in nonlinear constrained optimization.
   a. Thing
   b. Lagrange multipliers0
   c. Undefined
   d. Undefined

5. _____ is a process of combining or accumulating. It may also refer to:
   a. Integration0
   b. Thing
   c. Undefined
   d. Undefined

6. _____ of a function of several variables is its derivative with respect to one of those variables with the others held constant as opposed to the total derivative, in which all variables are allowed to vary.

Chapter 7. Functions of Several Variables

  a. Partial derivative0
  b. Thing
  c. Undefined
  d. Undefined

7. The _____ is a measurement of how a function changes when the values of its inputs change.
  a. Derivative0
  b. Thing
  c. Undefined
  d. Undefined

8. The mathematical concept of a _____ expresses the intuitive idea of deterministic dependence between two quantities, one of which is viewed as primary and the other as secondary. A _____ then is a way to associate a unique output for each input of a specified type, for example, a real number or an element of a given set.
  a. Function0
  b. Thing
  c. Undefined
  d. Undefined

9. A _____ is 360° or 2δ radians.
  a. Thing
  b. Turn0
  c. Undefined
  d. Undefined

10. _____, from Latin meaning "to make progress", is defined in two different ways. Pure economic _____ is the increase in wealth that an investor has from making an investment, taking into consideration all costs associated with that investment including the opportunity cost of capital.
  a. Profit0
  b. Thing
  c. Undefined
  d. Undefined

11. Acid _____ ratio measures the ability of a company to use its near cash or quick assets to immediately extinguish its current liabilities.

Chapter 7. Functions of Several Variables

a. Test0
b. Thing
c. Undefined
d. Undefined

12. In mathematics, the conjugate _____ or adjoint matrix of an m-by-n matrix A with complex entries is the n-by-m matrix A* obtained from A by taking the transpose and then taking the complex conjugate of each entry.
   a. Pairs0
   b. Thing
   c. Undefined
   d. Undefined

13. In mathematics, a _____ is a two-dimensional manifold or surface that is perfectly flat.
   a. Plane0
   b. Thing
   c. Undefined
   d. Undefined

14. In mathematics, a _____ of a k-place relation $L \subseteq X_1 \times \ldots \times X_k$ is one of the sets X_j, $1 \leq j \leq k$. In the special case where k = 2 and $L \subseteq X_1 \times X_2$ is a function $L : X_1 \to X_2$, it is conventional to refer to X_1 as the _____ of the function and to refer to X_2 as the codomain of the function.
   a. Domain0
   b. Thing
   c. Undefined
   d. Undefined

15. An _____ is a collection of two not necessarily distinct objects, one of which is distinguished as the first coordinate and the other as the second coordinate.
   a. Thing
   b. Ordered pair0
   c. Undefined
   d. Undefined

16. _____ is the ability to hold, receive or absorb, or a measure thereof, similar to the concept of volume.

Chapter 7. Functions of Several Variables

a. Concept
b. Capacity0
c. Undefined
d. Undefined

17. A _____ is a quantity that denotes the proportional amount or magnitude of one quantity relative to another.
a. Thing
b. Ratio0
c. Undefined
d. Undefined

18. _____ is the application of tools and a processing medium to the transformation of raw materials into finished goods for sale.
a. Manufacturing0
b. Thing
c. Undefined
d. Undefined

19. U.S. liquid _____ is legally defined as 231 cubic inches, and is equal to 3.785411784 litres or abotu 0.13368 cubic feet. This is the most common definition of a _____. The U.S. fluid ounce is defined as 1/128 of a U.S. _____.
a. Gallon0
b. Thing
c. Undefined
d. Undefined

20. In sociology and biology a _____ is the collection of people or organisms of a particular species living in a given geographic area or space, usually measured by a census.
a. Thing
b. Population0
c. Undefined
d. Undefined

21. A _____ is a unit of length, usually used to measure distance, in a number of different systems, including Imperial units, United States customary units and Norwegian/Swedish mil. Its size can vary from system to system, but in each is between 1 and 10 kilometers. In contemporary English contexts _____ refers to either:

Chapter 7. Functions of Several Variables

a. Mile0
b. Thing
c. Undefined
d. Undefined

22. In mathematics, an _____, mean, or central tendency of a data set refers to a measure of the "middle" or "expected" value of the data set.
a. Concept
b. Average0
c. Undefined
d. Undefined

23. In mathematics and the mathematical sciences, a _____ is a fixed, but possibly unspecified, value. This is in contrast to a variable, which is not fixed.
a. Thing
b. Constant0
c. Undefined
d. Undefined

24. _____ is a function whose values do not vary and thus are constant.
a. Constant function0
b. Thing
c. Undefined
d. Undefined

25. In mathematics, the _____ of a coordinate system is the point where the axes of the system intersect.
a. Thing
b. Origin0
c. Undefined
d. Undefined

26. In geometry, two lines or planes if one falls on the other in such a way as to create congruent adjacent angles. The term may be used as a noun or adjective. Thus, referring to Figure 1, the line AB is the _____ to CD through the point B.

a. Thing
b. Perpendicular0
c. Undefined
d. Undefined

27. _____ are the basic objects of study in graph theory. Informally speaking, a graph is a set of objects called points, nodes, or vertices connected by links called lines or edges.
a. Graphs0
b. Thing
c. Undefined
d. Undefined

28. _____, or EPS are the earnings returned on the initial investment amount.
a. Earnings per share0
b. Thing
c. Undefined
d. Undefined

29. Mathematical _____ is used to represent ideas.
a. Thing
b. Notation0
c. Undefined
d. Undefined

30. _____ is the writing of numbers in the base-ten numeral system, which uses various symbols called digits for ten distinct values 0, 1, 2, 3, 4, 5, 6, 7, 8 and 9 to represent numbers
a. Thing
b. Decimal notation0
c. Undefined
d. Undefined

31. _____ is a payment made by a company to its shareholders

Chapter 7. Functions of Several Variables

a. Dividend0
b. Thing
c. Undefined
d. Undefined

32. _____ is a way of expressing a number as a fraction of 100 per cent meaning "per hundred".
a. Percent0
b. Thing
c. Undefined
d. Undefined

33. In geometry, the _____ of an object is a point in some sense in the middle of the object.
a. Thing
b. Center0
c. Undefined
d. Undefined

34. In classical geometry, a _____ of a circle or sphere is any line segment from its center to its boundary. By extension, the _____ of a circle or sphere is the length of any such segment. The _____ is half the diameter. In science and engineering the term _____ of curvature is commonly used as a synonym for _____.
a. Radius0
b. Thing
c. Undefined
d. Undefined

35. The _____ of a solid object is the three-dimensional concept of how much space it occupies, often quantified numerically.
a. Thing
b. Volume0
c. Undefined
d. Undefined

36. _____ is a term applied when talking about the movement of air from one place to the next.

a. Wind speed0
b. Thing
c. Undefined
d. Undefined

37. _____ is a unit of speed, expressing the number of international miles covered per hour.
a. Miles per hour0
b. Thing
c. Undefined
d. Undefined

38. The _____ or kilogramme is the SI base unit of mass. It is defined as being equal to the mass of the international prototype of the _____.
a. Kilogram0
b. Thing
c. Undefined
d. Undefined

39. In mathematics, a _____ is the end result of a division problem. It can also be expressed as the number of times the divisor divides into the dividend.
a. Quotient0
b. Thing
c. Undefined
d. Undefined

40. An _____ is a score derived from one of several different standardized tests attempting to measure intelligence.
a. Thing
b. Intelligence Quotient0
c. Undefined
d. Undefined

41. _____ is the fee paid on borrowed money.

Chapter 7. Functions of Several Variables 165

a. Interest0
b. Thing
c. Undefined
d. Undefined

42. _____ is a physical property of a system that underlies the common notions of hot and cold; something that is hotter has the greater _____.
a. Thing
b. Temperature0
c. Undefined
d. Undefined

43. _____ is a temperature scale named after the German physicist Daniel Gabriel _____ , who proposed it in 1724.
a. Thing
b. Fahrenheit0
c. Undefined
d. Undefined

44. In mathematics, there are several meanings of _____ depending on the subject.
a. Thing
b. Degree0
c. Undefined
d. Undefined

45. An _____ is a combination of numbers, operators, grouping symbols and/or free variables and bound variables arranged in a meaningful way which can be evaluated..
a. Thing
b. Expression0
c. Undefined
d. Undefined

46. In mathematics, the concept of a _____ tries to capture the intuitive idea of a geometrical one-dimensional and continuous object. A simple example is the circle.

166 Chapter 7. Functions of Several Variables

   a. Thing
   b. Curve0
   c. Undefined
   d. Undefined

47. _____ is often used to describe the measurement of the steepness, incline, gradient, or grade of a straight line. The _____ is defined as the ratio of the "rise" divided by the "run" between two points on a line, or in other words, the ratio of the altitude change to the horizontal distance between any two points on the line.
   a. Thing
   b. Slope0
   c. Undefined
   d. Undefined

48. In trigonometry, the _____ is a function defined as $\tan x = \sin x / \cos x$. The function is so-named because it can be defined as the length of a certain segment of a _____ (in the geometric sense) to the unit circle. In plane geometry, a line is _____ to a curve, at some point, if both line and curve pass through the point with the same direction.
   a. Tangent0
   b. Thing
   c. Undefined
   d. Undefined

49. _____ has two distinct but etymologically-related meanings: one in geometry and one in trigonometry.
   a. Tangent line0
   b. Thing
   c. Undefined
   d. Undefined

50. _____ asserts that the maximum output of a technologically-determined production process is a mathematical function of input factors of production.
   a. Production function0
   b. Thing
   c. Undefined
   d. Undefined

51. The _____ of measurement are a globally standardized and modernized form of the metric system.

Chapter 7. Functions of Several Variables 167

a. Units0
b. Thing
c. Undefined
d. Undefined

52. _____, in economics and political economy, are the distributions or payments awarded to the various suppliers of the factors of production.
a. Thing
b. Returns0
c. Undefined
d. Undefined

53. According to _____ relationship, in a production system with fixed and variable inputs, beyond some point, each additional unit of variable input yields less and less additional output.
a. Thing
b. Diminishing returns0
c. Undefined
d. Undefined

54. A _____ is a compensation which workers receive in exchange for their labor.
a. Thing
b. Wage0
c. Undefined
d. Undefined

55. A _____ is a special kind of ratio, indicating a relationship between two measurements with different units, such as miles to gallons or cents to pounds.
a. Thing
b. Rate0
c. Undefined
d. Undefined

56. In plane geometry, a _____ is a polygon with four equal sides, four right angles, and parallel opposite sides. In algebra, the _____ of a number is that number multiplied by itself.

a. Square0
b. Thing
c. Undefined
d. Undefined

57. _____ is a state located in the southern and southwestern regions of the United States of America.
a. Thing
b. Texas0
c. Undefined
d. Undefined

58. _____ studies and addresses the ways in which individuals, businesses, and organizations raise, allocate, and use monetary resources over time, taking into account the risks entailed in their projects
a. Finance0
b. Thing
c. Undefined
d. Undefined

59. _____ is a set, with some particular properties and usually some additional structure, such as the operations of addition or multiplication, for instance.
a. Space0
b. Thing
c. Undefined
d. Undefined

60. The word _____ is used in a variety of ways in mathematics.
a. Index0
b. Thing
c. Undefined
d. Undefined

61. _____ is a kind of property which exists as magnitude or multitude. It is among the basic classes of things along with quality, substance, change, and relation.

Chapter 7. Functions of Several Variables

a. Thing
b. Amount0
c. Undefined
d. Undefined

62. _____, a field in mathematics, is the study of how functions change when their inputs change. The primary object of study in _____ is the derivative.
a. Differential calculus0
b. Thing
c. Undefined
d. Undefined

63. in mathematics, maxima and minima, known collectively as _____, are the largest value maximum or smallest value minimum, that a function takes in a point either within a given neighborhood or on the function domain in its entirety global extremum.
a. Thing
b. Extrema0
c. Undefined
d. Undefined

64. The _____ is the highest point in a certain portion of a graph.
a. Relative maximum0
b. Thing
c. Undefined
d. Undefined

65. The _____ is the lowest point in a certain portion of a graph.
a. Thing
b. Relative minimum0
c. Undefined
d. Undefined

66. In the most general terms, a _____ for a smooth function (curve, surface or hypersurface) is a point such that the curve/surface/etc. in the neighborhood of this point lies on different sides of the tangent at this point. In certain contexts the definition may vary. It is most frequently used at critical points.

Chapter 7. Functions of Several Variables

   a. Thing
   b. Saddle point0
   c. Undefined
   d. Undefined

67. _____ determines whether a given stationary point of a function is a maximum or a minimum.
   a. Thing
   b. Second derivative test0
   c. Undefined
   d. Undefined

68. _____ is a point on the domain of a function
   a. Critical point0
   b. Thing
   c. Undefined
   d. Undefined

69. The word _____ means curving in or hollowed inward.
   a. Thing
   b. Concavity0
   c. Undefined
   d. Undefined

70. A _____ is the sum of the elements of a sequence.
   a. Thing
   b. Series0
   c. Undefined
   d. Undefined

71. _____ are external two-dimensional outlines, with the appearance or configuration of some thing - in contrast to the matter or content or substance of which it is composed.

Chapter 7. Functions of Several Variables

a. Thing
b. Shapes0
c. Undefined
d. Undefined

72. A _____ can refer to a line joining two nonadjacent vertices of a polygon or polyhedron, or in some contexts any upward or downward sloping line. .
a. Diagonal0
b. Thing
c. Undefined
d. Undefined

73. In economics, economic _____ is simply a state of the world where economic forces are balanced and in the absence of external influences the values of economic variables will not change.
a. Equilibrium0
b. Thing
c. Undefined
d. Undefined

74. In mathematics, suppose C is a collection of mathematical objects . Then we say that C is _____ if every c ∊ C is uniquely determined by less information about c than one would expect.
a. Rigid0
b. Thing
c. Undefined
d. Undefined

75. _____ is a reaction force applied by a stretched string on the objects which stretch it.
a. Tension0
b. Thing
c. Undefined
d. Undefined

76. A _____ is a negotiable instrument instructing a financial institution to pay a specific amount of a specific currency from a specific demand account held in the maker/depositor's name with that institution. Both the maker and payee may be natural persons or legal entities.

a. Thing
b. Check0
c. Undefined
d. Undefined

77. _____ is a business term for the amount of money that a company receives from its activities in a given period, mostly from sales of products and/or services to customers
a. Thing
b. Revenue0
c. Undefined
d. Undefined

78. In mathematics, a _____ is the result of multiplying, or an expression that identifies factors to be multiplied.
a. Product0
b. Thing
c. Undefined
d. Undefined

79. A _____ is a set of numbers that designate location in a given reference system, such as x,y in a planar _____ system or an x,y,z in a three-dimensional _____ system.
a. Coordinate0
b. Thing
c. Undefined
d. Undefined

80. _____ is a synonym for information.
a. Data0
b. Thing
c. Undefined
d. Undefined

81. In economics, supply and _____ describe market relations between prospective sellers and buyers of a good.

Chapter 7. Functions of Several Variables 173

   a. Thing
   b. Demand0
   c. Undefined
   d. Undefined

82. _____ or life assurance is a contract between the policy owner and the insurer, where the insurer agrees to pay a sum of money upon the occurrence of the policy owner's death.
   a. Life insurance0
   b. Thing
   c. Undefined
   d. Undefined

83. _____, in law and economics, is a form of risk management primarily used to hedge against the risk of a contingent loss.
   a. Insurance0
   b. Thing
   c. Undefined
   d. Undefined

84. In physics, _____ is an influence that may cause an object to accelerate. It may be experienced as a lift, a push, or a pull. The actual acceleration of the body is determined by the vector sum of all forces acting on it, known as net _____ or resultant _____.
   a. Thing
   b. Force0
   c. Undefined
   d. Undefined

85. An _____ is an increase, either of some fixed amount, for example added regularly, or of a variable amount.
   a. Increment0
   b. Thing
   c. Undefined
   d. Undefined

86. _____ the expected value of a random variable displays the average or central value of the variable. It is a summary value of the distribution of the variable.

Chapter 7. Functions of Several Variables

　a. Thing
　b. Determining0
　c. Undefined
　d. Undefined

87. _____ is a measure of difference for interval and ratio variables between the observed value and the mean.
　a. Deviation0
　b. Thing
　c. Undefined
　d. Undefined

88. A _____ is the result of the addition of a set of numbers. The numbers may be natural numbers, complex numbers, matrices, or still more complicated objects. An infinite _____ is a subtle procedure known as a series.
　a. Thing
　b. Sum0
　c. Undefined
　d. Undefined

89. In regression analysis, _____, also known as ordinary _____ analysis is a method for linear regression that determines the values of unknown quantities in a statistical model by minimizing the sum of the residuals difference between the predicted and observed values squared.
　a. Least squares0
　b. Thing
　c. Undefined
　d. Undefined

90. The deductive-nomological model is a formalized view of scientific _____ in natural language.
　a. Thing
　b. Explanation0
　c. Undefined
　d. Undefined

91. A _____ is a statement or claimt that a particular event will occur in the future in more certain terms than a forecast.

Chapter 7. Functions of Several Variables 175

  a. Prediction0
  b. Thing
  c. Undefined
  d. Undefined

92. The word _____ comes from the Latin word linearis, which means created by lines.
  a. Linear0
  b. Thing
  c. Undefined
  d. Undefined

93. A _____ is an equation in which each term is either a constant or the product of a constant times the first power of a variable.
  a. Thing
  b. Linear equation0
  c. Undefined
  d. Undefined

94. In probability theory and statistics, _____, also called _____ coefficient, indicates the strength and direction of a linear relationship between two random variables.
  a. Correlation0
  b. Thing
  c. Undefined
  d. Undefined

95. In mathematics, a _____ is a constant multiplicative factor of a certain object. The object can be such things as a variable, a vector, a function, etc. For example, the _____ of $9x^2$ is 9.
  a. Coefficient0
  b. Thing
  c. Undefined
  d. Undefined

96. _____ indicates the strength and direction of a linear relationship between two random variables.

Chapter 7. Functions of Several Variables

   a. Coefficient of correlation0
   b. Thing
   c. Undefined
   d. Undefined

97. _____ is a statistical measure of the average length of survival of a living thing.
   a. Thing
   b. Life expectancy0
   c. Undefined
   d. Undefined

98. A _____ is a first degree polynomial mathematical function of the form: f(x) = mx + b where m and b are real constants and x is a real variable.
   a. Linear function0
   b. Thing
   c. Undefined
   d. Undefined

99. _____ is a regression method that models the relationship between a dependent variable Y, independent variables Xp, and a random term å.
   a. Thing
   b. Linear regression0
   c. Undefined
   d. Undefined

100. In mathematics, a _____ is a condition that a solution to an optimization problem must satisfy in order to be acceptable.
   a. Thing
   b. Constraint0
   c. Undefined
   d. Undefined

101. The _____, the average in everyday English, which is also called the arithmetic _____ (and is distinguished from the geometric _____ or harmonic _____). The average is also called the sample _____. The expected value of a random variable, which is also called the population _____.

Chapter 7. Functions of Several Variables

   a. Mean0
   b. Thing
   c. Undefined
   d. Undefined

102. A _____ is an individual or household that purchases and uses goods and services generated within the economy.
   a. Thing
   b. Consumer0
   c. Undefined
   d. Undefined

103. _____ is the distance around a given two-dimensional object. As a general rule, the _____ of a polygon can always be calculated by adding all the length of the sides together. So, the formula for triangles is P = a + b + c, where a, b and c stand for each side of it. For quadrilaterals the equation is P = a + b + c + d. For equilateral polygons, P = na, where n is the number of sides and a is the side length.
   a. Perimeter0
   b. Thing
   c. Undefined
   d. Undefined

104. Compass and straightedge or ruler-and-compass _____ is the _____ of lengths or angles using only an idealized ruler and compass.
   a. Construction0
   b. Thing
   c. Undefined
   d. Undefined

105. _____ represents the combinations of goods and services that a consumer can purchase given current prices and his income.
   a. Budget constraint0
   b. Thing
   c. Undefined
   d. Undefined

Chapter 7. Functions of Several Variables

106. _____, was an Italian mathematician and astronomer who created the calculus of variations which was later expanded by Weierstrass, solved the isoperimetrical problem on which the variational calculus is based in part.
   a. Person
   b. Joseph Louis Lagrange0
   c. Undefined
   d. Undefined

107. The _____ of a function is an extension of the concept of a sum, and are identified or found through the use of integration.
   a. Integral0
   b. Thing
   c. Undefined
   d. Undefined

108. In mathematics, a matrix can be thought of as each row or _____ being a vector. Hence, a space formed by row vectors or _____ vectors are said to be a row space or a _____ space.
   a. Column0
   b. Concept
   c. Undefined
   d. Undefined

109. In mathematics, _____ geometry was the traditional name for the geometry of three-dimensional Euclidean space — for practical purposes the kind of space we live in.
   a. Thing
   b. Solid0
   c. Undefined
   d. Undefined

110. In mathematical analysis and related areas of mathematics, a set is called _____, if it is, in a certain sense, of finite size.
   a. Bounded0
   b. Thing
   c. Undefined
   d. Undefined

111. In mathematics, a _____ is an n-tuple with n being 3.

a. Triple0
b. Thing
c. Undefined
d. Undefined

112. A frame of _____ is a particular perspective from which the universe is observed.
a. Reference0
b. Thing
c. Undefined
d. Undefined

113. _____ are activities that are governed by a set of rules or customs and often engaged in competitively.
a. Thing
b. Sports0
c. Undefined
d. Undefined

114. _____ is the transport of people on a trip/journey or the process or time involved in a person or object moving from one location to another.
a. Thing
b. Travel0
c. Undefined
d. Undefined

115. In astronomy, geography, geometry and related sciences and contexts, a plane is said to be _____ at a given point if it is locally perpendicular to the gradient of the gravity field, i.e., with the direction of the gravitational force at that point.
a. Horizontal0
b. Thing
c. Undefined
d. Undefined

Chapter 1

1. b	2. b	3. b	4. b	5. a	6. b	7. a	8. a	9. a	10. a
11. b	12. a	13. a	14. a	15. a	16. a	17. a	18. b	19. b	20. b
21. a	22. b	23. a	24. b	25. a	26. b	27. a	28. a	29. b	30. b
31. a	32. b	33. a	34. a	35. a	36. a	37. a	38. b	39. b	40. a
41. a	42. a	43. b	44. a	45. b	46. b	47. a	48. a	49. b	50. b
51. b	52. a	53. b	54. b	55. b	56. a	57. b	58. a	59. b	60. a
61. b	62. b	63. b	64. b	65. a	66. b	67. a	68. a	69. b	70. a
71. b	72. a	73. a	74. a	75. b	76. b	77. a	78. a	79. b	80. b
81. b	82. b	83. a	84. b	85. b	86. b	87. a	88. b	89. a	90. a
91. b	92. a	93. a	94. b	95. a	96. a	97. a	98. b	99. a	100. a
101. a	102. b	103. b	104. b	105. b	106. b	107. b	108. a	109. b	110. b
111. a	112. b	113. a	114. b	115. b	116. a	117. b	118. b	119. b	120. a
121. b	122. a	123. b	124. b	125. b	126. a	127. b	128. a	129. b	130. b
131. b	132. a	133. b	134. a	135. b	136. a	137. b	138. b	139. b	140. b
141. b	142. b	143. a	144. a	145. b	146. a	147. b	148. b	149. a	150. b
151. b									

Chapter 2

1. a	2. a	3. a	4. a	5. b	6. a	7. a	8. b	9. b	10. a
11. a	12. a	13. b	14. a	15. b	16. b	17. a	18. b	19. b	20. b
21. b	22. b	23. b	24. a	25. a	26. b	27. a	28. b	29. a	30. a
31. a	32. a	33. b	34. b	35. a	36. a	37. b	38. b	39. a	40. a
41. b	42. a	43. b	44. a	45. b	46. a	47. a	48. b	49. a	50. b
51. b	52. b	53. b	54. b	55. b	56. b	57. b	58. a	59. b	60. a
61. a	62. b	63. a	64. b	65. a	66. a	67. a	68. b	69. b	70. b
71. b	72. a	73. b	74. a	75. a	76. b	77. b	78. a	79. a	80. a
81. a	82. b	83. b	84. a	85. b	86. b	87. a	88. a	89. b	90. a
91. a	92. b	93. a	94. a	95. a	96. a	97. b	98. a	99. b	100. b
101. b	102. b	103. a	104. a	105. a	106. a	107. a	108. a	109. a	110. a
111. a	112. a	113. b	114. a	115. b	116. b	117. a	118. b	119. b	120. a
121. a	122. b	123. a	124. a	125. b	126. b				

ANSWER KEY

Chapter 3

1. b	2. b	3. b	4. a	5. b	6. a	7. b	8. b	9. a	10. a
11. a	12. a	13. a	14. a	15. a	16. a	17. b	18. b	19. a	20. b
21. a	22. a	23. a	24. a	25. a	26. b	27. b	28. a	29. b	30. a
31. b	32. a	33. b	34. a	35. a	36. a	37. a	38. a	39. a	40. b
41. b	42. a	43. b	44. a	45. b	46. a	47. a	48. a	49. b	50. a
51. a	52. b	53. a	54. a	55. a	56. a	57. a	58. b	59. a	60. a
61. a	62. b	63. b	64. a	65. a	66. b	67. a	68. a	69. a	70. b
71. b	72. b	73. a	74. a	75. a	76. a	77. b	78. a	79. a	80. b
81. b	82. b	83. b	84. a	85. b	86. a	87. a	88. b	89. a	90. b
91. b	92. a	93. b	94. a	95. a	96. a	97. b	98. b	99. a	100. b
101. a	102. b	103. b	104. b	105. a	106. b	107. a	108. a	109. a	110. b
111. b	112. a	113. a	114. b	115. b	116. a	117. b	118. a	119. b	120. b
121. a	122. b	123. a	124. a	125. a	126. a	127. b	128. b	129. a	130. a
131. b	132. b	133. a	134. a	135. a	136. a	137. a	138. b		

Chapter 4

1. b	2. b	3. b	4. b	5. a	6. a	7. b	8. b	9. a	10. b
11. a	12. b	13. b	14. a	15. a	16. a	17. b	18. b	19. b	20. b
21. a	22. b	23. b	24. b	25. a	26. b	27. b	28. b	29. a	30. a
31. b	32. b	33. b	34. a	35. a	36. b	37. a	38. a	39. b	40. a
41. a	42. b	43. a	44. b	45. b	46. b	47. a	48. b	49. b	50. b
51. a	52. a	53. a	54. b	55. b	56. a	57. b	58. a	59. a	60. b
61. a	62. b	63. b	64. b	65. b	66. a	67. a	68. b	69. a	70. a
71. b	72. b	73. b	74. b	75. b	76. a	77. b	78. b	79. b	80. a
81. b	82. a	83. b	84. b	85. b	86. b	87. a	88. b	89. a	90. b
91. a	92. b	93. a	94. a	95. a	96. a	97. a	98. a	99. a	100. a
101. a	102. b	103. b	104. b	105. a	106. b	107. b	108. b	109. b	110. a
111. a	112. a	113. a	114. a	115. a	116. b	117. a	118. a	119. a	120. b
121. a	122. b	123. a	124. a	125. b	126. a	127. a	128. b	129. b	130. b
131. b	132. a	133. a							

Chapter 5

1. b	2. b	3. b	4. b	5. b	6. b	7. a	8. b	9. a	10. b
11. a	12. b	13. a	14. a	15. a	16. a	17. a	18. a	19. a	20. a
21. b	22. b	23. b	24. b	25. a	26. a	27. b	28. a	29. b	30. a
31. a	32. a	33. b	34. b	35. a	36. a	37. a	38. b	39. a	40. b
41. b	42. a	43. a	44. a	45. b	46. a	47. b	48. a	49. b	50. b
51. b	52. b	53. b	54. a	55. b	56. a	57. b	58. a	59. a	60. a
61. a	62. b	63. b	64. b	65. b	66. a	67. a	68. b	69. b	70. b
71. a	72. a	73. b	74. a	75. b	76. b	77. b	78. a	79. a	80. a
81. b	82. b	83. b	84. a	85. b	86. b	87. b	88. b	89. b	90. a
91. b	92. b	93. a	94. a	95. b	96. a				

Chapter 6

1. b	2. b	3. a	4. b	5. b	6. b	7. b	8. b	9. b	10. a
11. a	12. a	13. b	14. a	15. b	16. a	17. a	18. b	19. b	20. b
21. a	22. b	23. b	24. b	25. b	26. b	27. a	28. b	29. b	30. b
31. a	32. b	33. a	34. a	35. a	36. a	37. a	38. a	39. b	40. b
41. b	42. b	43. b	44. b	45. a	46. b	47. a	48. a	49. a	50. a
51. a	52. b	53. b	54. b	55. b	56. a	57. a	58. b	59. a	60. a
61. b	62. a	63. b	64. a	65. a	66. a	67. b	68. b	69. a	70. a
71. b	72. a	73. b	74. b	75. a	76. a	77. a	78. b	79. a	80. a
81. a	82. b	83. a	84. a	85. a	86. a	87. b	88. a	89. b	90. a
91. b	92. a	93. b	94. a	95. b	96. b	97. b	98. b	99. b	100. b
101. b	102. b	103. b	104. b	105. b	106. b	107. b	108. b	109. a	110. a
111. b	112. a	113. a	114. a	115. a					

Chapter 7

1. a	2. a	3. b	4. b	5. a	6. a	7. a	8. a	9. b	10. a
11. a	12. a	13. a	14. a	15. b	16. b	17. b	18. a	19. a	20. b
21. a	22. b	23. b	24. a	25. b	26. b	27. a	28. a	29. b	30. b
31. a	32. a	33. b	34. a	35. b	36. a	37. a	38. a	39. a	40. b
41. a	42. b	43. b	44. b	45. b	46. b	47. b	48. a	49. a	50. a
51. a	52. b	53. b	54. b	55. b	56. a	57. b	58. a	59. a	60. a
61. b	62. a	63. b	64. a	65. b	66. b	67. b	68. a	69. b	70. b
71. b	72. a	73. a	74. a	75. a	76. b	77. b	78. a	79. a	80. a
81. b	82. a	83. a	84. b	85. a	86. b	87. a	88. b	89. a	90. b
91. a	92. a	93. b	94. a	95. a	96. a	97. b	98. a	99. b	100. b
101. a	102. b	103. a	104. a	105. a	106. b	107. a	108. a	109. b	110. a
111. a	112. a	113. b	114. b	115. a					